The 20 British Prime Ministers
of the 20th century

Thatcher

CLARE BECKETT

HAUS PUBLISHING · LONDON

First published in Great Britain in 2006 by
Haus Publishing Limited
26 Cadogan Court
Draycott Avenue
London SW3 3BX

www.hauspublishing.co.uk

Copyright © Clare Beckett, 2006

The moral right of the author has been asserted

A CIP catalogue record for this book is available from the British Library

ISBN 1-904950-71-X

Designed by BrillDesign
Typeset in Garamond 3 by MacGuru Ltd
info@macguru.org.uk

Printed and bound by Graphicom, Vicenza

Front cover: John Holder

Contents

Part One

THE LIFE

Chapter 1: Mr Roberts' Daughter

It was an ordinary day in Grantham. On 13 October 1925, very little of note happened there, except that Margaret Hilda Roberts was born. She describes her first memories as an idyllic blur *in which the sun was always shining through the leaves of the lime tree into our living room and someone – my mother, my sister, one of the people working in the shop – was always nearby to cuddle me or pacify me with a sweet.*[1] For she was born above her father's grocery shop.

The family were already established in business when Margaret Roberts arrived. Her father, Alfred Roberts, was a grey-haired and pious Alderman of the town. He was a self-made man, the son of a shoemaker who had left school at 13. He went into the grocery trade, at first working in the 'tuck shop' at Oundle School, and later managing a grocery store in Grantham. He had made many attempts to enlist in the army during the First World War, but had been turned down on medical grounds. His younger brother Edward did serve, and died at Salonika in 1917.

That year, Alfred Roberts married Beatrice Ethel Stephenson. They met through the local Methodist community, and were married in the church – the same one that Margaret Roberts attended regularly throughout her childhood. Beatrice Stephenson was a successful dressmaker. She was as frugal and practical as her husband, and they set out to save

and prosper. In 1919, they took out a mortgage on a shop in North Parade. It was well placed, on a crossroads, near to the railway line: Margaret Roberts must have been able to set her watch by the sound of the trains. Pictures show a large Edwardian building. Nowadays, some of these big, comfortable houses have become guesthouses. Margaret Roberts regretted that there was no garden, though.

By 1921, when Margaret's sister Muriel was born, the family were comfortably settled. This was not sufficient for Alfred Roberts. He was a careful and prudent man, with ambition that his family should never suffer as he did in his own impoverished childhood. He was determined to build a solid and, if possible, wealthy base for his family, where his daughters could grow to live a full and useful life. In 1923, he opened a second shop in Huntingdon Road. In 1925 he expanded his business into two adjoining properties in North Parade.

Prosperity did not lead to unnecessary expenditure, however. Margaret Roberts was born into a *home that was practical, serious and intensely religious*.[2] In the mid-1930s, 75 per cent of all families were officially designated working class but the Roberts, with two shops, were among the 20 per cent who could be considered middle class. Despite this the daughters had few possessions. There were no bicycles and not many toys, and trips to the theatre or cinema were rare. Their lives revolved around Methodism. The family went to Sunday morning service at 11.00, after Sunday school. There was Sunday school again in the afternoon, and the adults at least would attend service again in the evening.

Nonetheless, these early years were happy ones for Margaret Roberts. The shops were quality grocers, selling food more often found in delicatessens nowadays. Margaret helped behind the counter when she was old enough, and took a full part in measuring and packing sugar, coffee or tea for sale: these arrived in big bags, and had to be decanted into 1lb. weights. The family had some standing in the town, and Mr Roberts' younger daughter would have seen friendly faces and been made welcome wherever she went. She was part of the work upstairs, too – the unremitting work of making good and mending, washing and polishing, that kept a household respectable in the days before domestic appliances. She knew how to iron fine linen, and to heat a flat iron without scorching the linen. There is some triumph in running a comfortable, clean, and economic household that becomes a reward in itself. Thriftiness becomes competitive. Margaret Roberts describes finding out that another family saved and re-used their tacking cotton while dressmaking: from that point on she and her mother did the same.

Grantham, then as now, was a quiet, self-contained backwater. A small town rather than a city, it was neither flourishing nor depressed. But in the inter-war years the spectre of poverty was never very far away. Even people like Alfred Roberts, who had pulled himself up by his bootstraps and acquired a nest-egg, lived in fear that some accident or disaster would hit his family. These were the years before the welfare state, where even calling in the doctor was an expensive decision, so small provincial towns developed their own networks of support. The Roberts' shops made up to 150 parcels for the old and sick, bought by the local Rotarian Society. The Roberts' daughters attended and helped at town functions, and raised money for needy children. As grocers, the family knew something of the circumstances of their customers and community. Help was given to those who helped themselves. Later, Margaret Roberts described passing the long queue outside the dole office during the Great Depression. None of their close friends lost their jobs, but they knew people among the unemployed. She was later to write: *And I have never forgotten – how neatly turned out the children of those unemployed families were. Their parents were determined to make the sacrifices that were necessary for them. The spirit of self-reliance and independence was very strong in even the poorest people of the East Midlands towns. It meant that they never dropped out of the community and, because others quietly gave what they could, the community remained together.*[3] My parents lived through these years in East London, and their lasting memories are less positive. Children were hungry, adults were hopeless, and homelessness was a constant threat. It is easy to see how Margaret Roberts' early view of poverty and the poor informed her attitude to welfare later on in her life.

The spirit of self-reliance and independence was very strong in even the poorest people of the East Midlands towns.

THATCHER

Forced to give up his own formal education at 13, Alfred Roberts took a keen interest in his daughters' schooling. Margaret went to Huntingtower Road Primary School, close to home but with a good reputation. She had learned to read at home, as many of her generation had, and tells about an incident at the age of five when she was asked to pronounce 'w-r-a-p'. She got it right, but was aware that she was always asked the 'hard ones'. She describes herself as being mystified by proverbs – her literal mind had real difficulty with such ideas as 'look before you leap' – why not look before you cross, a much more understandable idea, given the busy roads outside the school? And how can you have both that proverb, and 'he who hesitates is lost'?

Both girls attended Kesteven and Grantham Girls' School. This was small, only 350 pupils, in a different part of town. It was a grant-aided grammar school. Parents would normally have paid part of the fees, but Margaret secured a county scholarship. The trip to school and back, home for lunch, and back in the afternoon meant that young Margaret was walking up to four miles a day: public transport, or staying for lunch, would have been unacceptable expenses. The school had a good reputation, and was already sending a few girls each year to Oxford. The 'girls in blue' were a familiar sight in the streets of Grantham. The intake came from a wide area, and Margaret's best friend lived some distance away in a more rural area. Margaret Roberts would stay overnight on visits there, and walk in the country. During the war, the Camden Girls' School was evacuated to Grantham, and their 'girls in green' shared classrooms. This meant altering the times of the school day, and the sisters would sometimes have to attend in the afternoons or mornings, or at weekends. Regardless, homework must always be completed even if that meant working on a Sunday. Her school reports show hard work and commitment and constant slight improvement but not brilliance. Outside the classroom, she was a competent hockey player, but her favoured sports were solitary. She enjoyed swimming, and particularly walking.

The thrift learned at home continued at school. All girls, however well-off or academic, had to take domestic science for four years. Miss Williams was a quiet and dignified head teacher. On special occasions, like prize-giving, she wore soft and well-tailored silk but her message was a familiar one – never buy a cheap fur coat when a good wool coat is a better buy. Go for the best you can afford, but do not live outside your means. The message was a part of my childhood too, and will be familiar to many girls of this generation. Buy to last and to keep up appearances, but beware the cheap and ostentatious. There were other unmarried women earning a living among Margaret Roberts' school teachers. This was a generation who would have to leave the profession if they married.

Miss Harding, the history teacher, offered a passionate introduction to the subject. Years later, Margaret could recall her account of the Dardanelles campaign as she visited Gallipoli. Miss Kay, who taught chemistry, opened a new world of logic to the young Margaret, based on the new scientific discoveries of that time.

Alfred Roberts was already a school governor, and became chairman while his daughters attended the school. This was not the only area in which he supported their learning, sometimes in surprisingly liberal ways. Finding that Margaret had not read Walt Whitman at school, he immediately found her some of his work, an author and poet with a modern, and sometimes risqué, style. He was responsible for bringing home two library books each week for his daughter, as well as books for her mother and sister. Reading included classic authors like Jane Austen and Dickens, but also political works. She struggled, with his assistance, with the *Hibbert Journal*, a philosophical periodical. He expected her to discuss her reading and learning with him, and to adopt a critical stance. He took her to 'Extension Lectures' given by the University of Nottingham, and supported her in contributing to discussion. Even as a young girl, she was used to stating her opinion and asking questions in an adult forum, and to arguing with the Alderman as a basis for learning. Perhaps it was these influences that lead to the one area where Margaret Roberts shone at school, as a member of the debating society. She was an unselfconscious star of debate, not brilliant, but logical and determined. Contemporaries remember her as hard to beat. Visiting speakers could always be sure of a question from her, slow and well-phrased with a Lincolnshire accent, delivered in a ringing and absolutely audible voice.

There was one major event during this quiet and hardworking childhood. Margaret's much-loved grandmother died when she was ten. Grandmother Stevenson was a formidable woman. Dressed in black sateen, she upheld Methodist values and was the first to condemn frivolity in any form. She was also a warm presence in the children's lives, telling bedtime stories and stories of life during her childhood. She had a spine-chilling line in ghost stories, told in the bedroom at night. She was a fund of old cautionary tales, like the ability of earwigs to crawl under your skin and form carbuncles. She had time for the girls as other members of the family had not, and often took part in the lighter tasks given to the children. Measuring spices, packing butter and light cleaning will all have been the kind of jobs assigned to the young and the old and shared by the two daughters and grandmother. When she died, Margaret and Muriel Roberts were sent to relatives until after the funeral and after Grandmother's things had been put away. This was the custom at that time, to shield children from death and disruption. After her death, the girls in the family began to attend the theatre and music halls occasionally.

This childhood was lived out against the rising shadow of economic slump and preparation for war. It would have been difficult for any intelligent and active child to ignore the changes around her, and impossible for the favoured daughter of a man who regarded public service as the rationale of life. Alfred was a councillor, Chairman of the Borough Finance Committee, Alderman and between 1945 and 1946 Mayor of Grantham. He was Alderman again in 1952, when he lost the position to a Labour candidate. Margaret Roberts' life was punctuated by elections and local events. 1935 stood out as an example, for this was the year of King George V's Jubilee and of Grantham's centenary as a borough. There were brass bands and decorations – Margaret says in her autobiography that the poorest part of town, Vere Street, was one of the best decorated. The boys' school and the girls' school combined for a big open-air display of marching and precision events, including forming the letters of Grantham. Margaret Roberts was part of the M.

To be part of local politics was only partly to be concerned with party politics. To Alfred, party politics had limits. He stood for the council as a ratepayer's candidate, believed in individual responsibility and sound financial management, and read John Stuart Mill. He described himself as a staunch Conservative. Labour councillors might argue with him in the council chamber, but they came to the shop without partisan bitterness. Margaret learned a lot of town business in the shop. General elections were a different matter. In 1935, the celebrations in the town were almost overshadowed by the first election in which Margaret was an active campaigner. She folded bright red leaflets for the Conservative candidate, sitting with much older companions. On election day, she was given responsibility for running between the office and the polling station with news about who had voted, and who still needed gathering in. This was a hard-fought election, and the member's majority was cut from 16,000 to 6,000. This election was fought in the inter-war period where most people wanted to avoid another war. The Roberts family read a wide variety of newspapers, and had a radio – they were probably better informed than most. The battle, though, was over the potential for and speed of disarmament. The Roberts family was not in favour of the policy of appease-ment of Hitler. It is not surprising that a fierce nationalism underpinned Alfred's Methodist politics of good husbandry and individual responsibility. For Margaret Roberts there was an added incentive. As a ten-year-old child, she says in her memoirs that she saw the monarchy as the glue that held society together and gave the poor the incentive to work hard and keep up appearances. While she seems to have had a worked-out view of poverty, learned from watching the customers in her fathers' shop, it is likely that her view of the Commonwealth reflected the Methodist values around her. Like many other families, the Roberts were fiercely proud of the Empire. Methodist ministry had been a foundation of colonisation, and the young Margaret Roberts listened to returning ministers with wonder. She would have liked to join the Indian civil service. She thought that the rule of law, good administration and order that the British had given to the colonies were great gifts.

In this period, Right and Left took on significant importance on the international stage. It was easy for right-wing people to be led into supporting fascism as a real alternative to communism. While the Roberts family hated communism, equally they did not find the strutting of the Blackshirts attractive. To them, surrounded by *the gentle self-regulation of our own civil life*,[4] only a free society was a possible alternative to both. They were not sanguine about another war. They saw the pictures of the First World War, and commemorated fallen servicemen, including Alfred's brother. The Remembrance Day parades were a constant reminder. They did not support appeasement, however. To them, Hitler was a significant and real threat who would not go away. He had crushed the Rotarians in Germany, and Alfred Roberts believed passionately in the power of Rotarian groups, their internationalism and their charity, as a force for good. With a rare flash of humour, Alfred felt that being destroyed by Hitler was the greatest compliment Rotary organisations could be paid. The local doctor was German, and received news that he passed to Alfred, who discussed it with Margaret. Muriel had a pen-friend in Austria, and after the *Anchluss* in 1938, the pen friend's father contacted the Roberts to see if they could take her in. Alfred arranged for the Grantham Rotarians to support her, and she stayed with each family in turn until she could go to relatives in South Africa. She brought first-hand experience of being Jewish under an anti-Semitic regime. One thing stuck in the young Margaret Roberts' mind – Jews were being made to scrub the streets. She was passionately anti-Hitler, unlike most of her neighbours at the time. She recounts standing in a chip-shop queue where the common opinion was that Hitler had at least brought some coherence to German policy and self-confidence to the German people. She argued against this opinion, although the queue was made up of adults.

To the Roberts' family, Hitler's wickedness must be ended, but the country was woefully unprepared. Margaret Roberts was nearly 14 on 3 September 1939, when war was finally declared. It was the only Sunday during her childhood that she did not go to church. It is typical of her approach in adulthood that in her autobiography she now turns to the social and political causes of war, rather than the privations that the war caused. Indeed, Grantham was not heavily bombed during the war. There were 21 air-raids on the town, and 78 people were killed. The greatest risk for the family was their closeness to the railway line, a few hundred yards from the house. Alfred was often out in the evenings on air-raid duty, while Margaret and her mother took shelter under the kitchen table. Muriel was already working at the orthopaedic hospital in Birmingham, where the bombing was much heavier. The Roberts family threw themselves into voluntary and civic work for the war effort, and were even busier than in peacetime.

Political life in Grantham did not stand still, however. In 1942, the town was the first to return a non-government candidate during the war. The Conservative, Sir Arthur

Longmore, lost his seat by 367 votes. Margaret Roberts was not involved in this campaign, and did not realise the lessons for the 1945 general election and the Labour landslide victory. She was preparing for entry to Oxford. She was taking the specific entry exam for Somerville College. She had earned her chance by hard work, not brilliance, and there is no sign in her memoirs that she was expecting or was expected to do this. Her entry may have been a result of wartime conditions, where more places were available to women. Certainly she was not a star pupil, and her entry had not been planned for. Although her school was sending a handful of girls to Oxford each year, Latin was required and she had not studied it before. It was not taught at the girls' grammar school, so she had to be 'crammed' by staff from the boys' school. She gave up learning the piano to keep up with the work. The scholarship mattered. The family would not be able, or possibly willing, to support her into higher education without it – there were no higher education grants for girls in the 1940s. Margaret had never been in any doubt that she would have to earn her own living as an adult. If she could not go to Oxford in 1943 she would have to study a two-year wartime degree, before being called up into service. At 17, and without Latin, the scholarship was a long shot and she failed. This was perhaps the first real and significant disappointment in her charmed and hard-working childhood. There was nothing for it but to enter the third-year sixth form, slightly cheered by becoming Joint Head of School. Then luck stepped in. Another candidate had dropped out – Margaret Roberts received a telegram offering her a place to be taken up immediately.

This was the end of Margaret Roberts' life in Grantham, the popular and favoured daughter of a well-known man. Her life was characterised by industry, thrift and civic duty. There were few frivolities, and no self-indulgent expenses. Alfred refused to have his house plumbed for hot water between the wars, judging it to be an unnecessary indulgence. His daughters carried water and bathed in hip tubs. Her world revolved around three friendly hubs – the family, the school and the church. Alfred's expectation was that she would work hard, and lead a useful and industrious life. The training he had given her in politics and argument stayed with her. Asked about her father, she would say *he gave me integrity*. His views were the core of the young Margaret Roberts' determination. This was not slavish orthodoxy, however. Alfred could, and did, bend with the wind without compromising his own principles. As a Methodist, he believed in keeping Sunday as a day of rest, but as a grocer, he worked. He voted for opening cinemas on Sunday, because the people attending bothered no-one but themselves, but he opposed opening parks on Sundays because games would create disturbance for others. He approved of the rhyme young Margaret Roberts learned at 11 from Bibby's Almanac:

'One ship drives east, and another drives west,
By the self same gale that blows;
'Tis the set of the sail, and not the gale,
That determines the way that she goes'
Ella Wheeler Wilcox[5]

He provided her with reading that covered classic and modern works and he shared her love of Kipling and of disciplined prose. He believed in the family as the foundation stone of a well-functioning society. He and his wife provided a stable and well-run home for his daughters.

It would be a mistake to think, however, that this was the only influence on her. Margaret Thatcher rarely spoke about her mother, but it was she who ran the home and set the routines. The backdrop to Margaret Roberts' life was a beautiful and well-kept home, surrounded by goods that were of the best quality the family could manage, and were cared for accordingly. Beatrice faded into the background of political and civic life, but was the source of the good clothes and disciplined behaviour that the family showed in public. She would take the girls on holiday to Skegness each year, and after her mother's death would also visit the theatre or cinema with her daughters. She will not have spent as much time in the company of her girls as many mothers – she helped run a thriving business and lived above the shop. She will have been available to the children when Alfred was busy, and will have been the power that made civic duties and entertaining possible.

Margaret Roberts herself shows a romantic, dreamy side to her character not connected to Alfred Roberts when she describes her childhood. She talks about her fascination with far-off countries, and her liking for the passionate and out-of-the-way insights in Kipling's poetry. She loved the theatre and music – even owning that one major attraction of Methodism was the music. She talks about a single trip to London with friends, where she fed the pigeons in Trafalgar Square, rode the Underground and visited the Zoo. At Kings Cross, she saw people from foreign countries, some in traditional dress, for the first time. The buildings, covered in soot, reminded this provincial child that she was at the centre of the world. But the high point of the trip – more than Downing Street or the Houses of Parliament, though they did not disappoint – was her first visit to the Catford Theatre in Lewisham to see *The Desert Song*. Margaret Roberts had little free time as a child, but what time she had was spent walking through the countryside alone, or reading poetry. At the age of ten, she won a prize at the Grantham Eisteddfod for reading John Drinkwater's *Moonlight Apples* and Walter de la Mare's *The Travellers*. Congratulated on her luck, she pointed out that she had worked very hard on the event. She and her mother played piano, and she sang in the choir. She looked forward to carol services, and sang in complicated productions like Mendelssohn's 'Elijah'. Altogether, growing up was hard work and discipline, but also liberal and joyous.

Margaret Roberts herself sums up the lessons she took with her to Oxford, and into her future life. *The first was that the kind of life that the people of Grantham had lived before the war was a decent and wholesome one, and its values were shaped by the community rather than the government. Second, since even a cultured, developed Christian country like Germany had fallen under Hitler's sway, civilisation could never be taken for granted and had to be constantly nurtured, which meant that good people had to stand up for the things they believed in. Third, I drew the obvious political conclusion that it was appeasement of dictators which had led to the war, and that had grown out of wrong-headed but decent principles, like the pacifism of Methodists in Grantham, as well as out of corrupt ones. One can never do without straightforward common sense in matters great as well as small. And finally I have to admit that I had the patriotic conviction that, given great leadership of the sort I heard from Winston Churchill in the radio broadcasts to which we listened, there was almost nothing that the British people could not do.*[6]

Chapter 2: Transitions

Oxford in wartime was not a place of dreaming spires. There were few people there from ordinary schools, or from small provincial towns like Grantham. Colleges were closed or merged, and many people who would expect to be undergraduates were either in the armed forces or dead. The average age of Margaret Roberts' contemporaries was 17½. The science facilities were dominated by war work – busy, but top secret and not available to a new undergraduate. At first, Margaret Roberts was dependent on her father's money, not on a scholarship, and was not used to being a small fish in a big pond. She was homesick and lonely. She was also, for the first time in her life, away from the backdrop of the Methodist church and civic duties. In modern times, this could be a recipe for disaster – disaffected students failing in their first year at university are commonplace. In wartime Oxford, the fear of being sent down was ever-present.

Margaret Roberts's first refuge was her work. She was not a brilliant chemist, and relied on hard work. Professor Dorothy Hodgkin, who taught her, says 'I came to rate her as good. One could always rely on her producing a sensible, well read essay.'[1] Good enough, at any rate, to choose Margaret Roberts as her research assistant during her fourth year at Oxford. Chemistry, like any discipline, forms the mind that studies it, and perhaps Chemistry, with its learning and logic leading to new conclusions was the perfect discipline for a Methodist given to flights of fancy. As Dorothy Hodgkin says of the study of chemistry and the human mind: 'I think it should interest you in the problems of finding out as much as you can about the way we work, the way matter is put together. And it should give you an interest in using the results.'[2]

The subject did offer Margaret Roberts genuine satisfaction. She particularly enjoyed the cutting edge of the discipline, and was excited by the advances in science driven by the war. This genuine interest led her to look for work in the science after 1947. She left Oxford with a Second Class degree in Chemistry, and approached the Oxford University Appointments Committee for a job. She had several unsuccessful interviews, and was finally taken on by BX Plastics, to work in their research and development section just outside Colchester. She had expected to be working as personal assistant to the research director, but that did not materialise. Instead, she donned her white lab coat as an active researcher. The section was new, and settled down around Margaret Roberts. She lived in Colchester, and travelled to work on the employer's bus. But the work was not satisfying, and Colchester, while pleasant, was scarcely less provincial than Grantham.

Side by side with her studies, Margaret Roberts became involved in student politics. For the first two years of her time at Oxford, the Oxford University Conservative Association (OUCA) was her club and second refuge. She worked, she took solitary walks round the town and country, and she socialised through the Conservative club. It is possible that at any other time in history a provincial tradesman's daughter would have found herself frozen out by sons and daughters of landowners bound together by public school. In 1943, Churchill's National Government was instrumental rather than ideological. The drivers of policy were the practical ones of munitions and soldiers, not the traditional ones of values and power. Conduct of the war dominated debate. Members of the Conservative Association were constrained in their social expectations and war work, and a young and civic-minded member could find friends and jobs that used her talents usefully. She could not join the Oxford Union, as membership was still denied to women. She could listen to the debates there, but the brittle and brilliant repartee of Union political debate was not for her. The Conservative Association offered a safer, quieter environment.

She made friends and contacts there that reappeared throughout her life. It was here that she met Edward Boyle, son of a wealthy Liberal MP, and William Rees-Mogg, future editor of *The Times*. The future broadcaster Robin Day was a leading light of the Oxford Union. Tony Benn – then the Honourable Anthony Wedgewood Benn – disagreed with Margaret Roberts on everything political. But she was welcome at the celebration when he became President of the Union, which, true to Methodist principle, was teetotal. Religion featured large in this period of her life. Methodism provided her with an anchor of stability reinforced by comforts brought from home – cakes and groceries to supplement rations and college fare, and a favourite armchair. She attended Sunday evening service at the Wesley Memorial Church, and went to the discussion suppers and social gatherings after that. She would attend the University Church of St Mary the Virgin for particular sermons, or the College Chapel if Helen Darbishire, College principal and Milton and Wordsworth scholar, was speaking. She did not attend Anglican churches, but she did read C S Lewis, the High Anglican and mystical writer. Again, this was a surprising path for a Methodist to take. However, Lewis does show that mix of idealism and practicality so liked by Margaret Roberts: 'Perfect behaviour may be as unattainable as perfect gear changing when we drive; but it is a necessary ideal prescribed for all men by the very nature of the human machine just as perfect gear changing is an ideal prescribed for all drivers by the very nature of cars.'[3] (This comment made more sense in the days when gear changes in cars required a complicated double use of the clutch.)

This quiet period was leading to the end of the war. Margaret Roberts spent two evenings of her week serving in the forces canteen at Carfax, giving her an awareness of service life. Elsewhere, preparations were beginning for the D-Day landings. In the Conservative Party, MPs who had last stood for election in 1935 were horrified by the extent to which the state now had control of industry. To them, it was vital to return to *laissez-faire* industry and free-market principles as soon as the war was over. On the other hand, young people were being demobilised from the forces, and looking towards a new Britain. Among these, Quintin Hogg was gathering support for reform of the party: 'If you don't give the people social reform, they are going to give you social revolution.'[4] He led a faction of modernists in the Conservative parliamentary party towards a platform of social reform previously unknown. The watershed in Margaret Roberts's quiet Oxford interlude came in 1945. Forced into an election against his wishes, Churchill stood as the victorious war leader against Clement Attlee, who had been part of the War Cabinet and now stood on a platform of welfare reform. Attlee was attractive to Margaret Roberts, who saw him as a careful and hard-working man. But his mandate was socialist and collectivist, and absolutely against her principles and beliefs.

'If you don't give the people social reform, they are going to give you social revolution.'

QUINTIN HOGG

This election was a landslide victory for Attlee. For young members of the Conservative Party like Margaret Roberts, this was the first experience of defeat on a national scale, and was a major wake-up call for the future. There had been other unsuccessful by-elections, like the one in Grantham, but the party had not heeded the warning these had given of the change in public opinion.

Margaret Roberts did not concede victory easily. In Oxford, she campaigned whole-heartedly for Quintin Hogg, although his belief in social reform was worrying. In Grantham, she was a 'warm-up' speaker for Conservative candidates in village meetings. She had received lessons in public speaking from Central Office – Mrs Stella Gatehouse emphasised simplicity, clarity of expression and a minimum of jargon. This gave her experience in handling crowds, although a little more long-windedness might have helped when candidates were late. Her views were clear – Germany should be disarmed and brought to justice, Churchill was best placed to continue to manage foreign affairs. There must be co-operation with America and hopefully with the Soviet Union. The British Empire, the *most important community of peoples the world had ever known* must never be dismembered.[5] None of this carried enough weight with the electorate. Decisions in this election were held over to enable serving troops to vote. Three weeks after polling day, Margaret Roberts was in Grantham when the results were announced. Conservative after Conservative fell, including the Grantham candidate. Margaret Roberts simply could not understand how the public could do this to Churchill. Only later did she begin to see it as a signal that change was in the air, rather than an act of disloyalty to a great leader.

This did, however, crystallise Margaret Roberts' political interests. In March 1946, she was Treasurer of the Oxford

University Conservative Association – by October she was elected President. In the meantime, she attended the Federation of University Conservative and Unionist Associations Conference in London. She spoke for the inclusion of more working-class people in Conservative politics – a speech that was noticed by the national party. She attended her first Conservative Party conference, in Blackpool. Back in Oxford she was organising, and meeting, speakers. Alec Douglas-Home, Anthony Eden, even Lady Davidson, who talked about being the only Conservative woman MP at the time. All of the leading Conservatives who worked the student circuit met Margaret Roberts, and she entertained as her father had entertained the great and the good of Grantham – without frills, and within the Association's means. She was central to the formation of a new manifesto for the Oxford Union Conservative Association – a manifesto committed to reform of the party. As a young Conservative – unusual at Somerville – she was invited to the principal's dinners when eminent guests were expected.

This was the position Margaret Roberts left when she moved to Colchester, and again became a small fish in a big pond. She did not leave her established base in politics, however. She had discovered what she really wanted to do with her life, and it was not chemistry. In her memoirs, she pinpoints a party at Corby Glen, a village some ten miles from Grantham, as the place where she first voiced her ambition. One of the men suggested that what she really wanted to do was to be an MP. Almost without thinking about it, she agreed – yes, that was what she really wanted to do.

She wasted no time in joining the local Conservative Association, and particularly the '39–45' discussion group of Conservatives of the war generation. She did not attempt to join the party's list of approved candidates. Alfred Roberts' daughter had no independent means, and could not have afforded to become an MP on the salaries offered at that time. Part of her campaign to increase middle-class representation in the party was to increase parliamentary salaries, and her arguments underpinned changes in the next few years. She kept in touch with friends made at University. She went to the Party Conference at Llandudno in 1948, as a representative of the University Graduate Conservative Association. The conference led to one of those accidents of parliamentary careers. A friend from Oxford was also a friend of the Chair of Dartford Conservative Association, who needed a candidate. The association 'had a look' at Margaret Roberts and in January 1949 she was selected. This was a mixed blessing – the Labour majority in that constituency was an unassailable 20,000. This may have worked in favour of the unknown female applicant – if there is no chance of winning, than why not give an unknown a chance? It did, however, spell the end of life in Colchester.

To fight the Dartford seat, her next job must be London based. She was looking for something that would pay about £500 per year – not an enormous amount, even in the cash-strapped 1950s. She had several refusals, but was eventually taken on by the laboratories of J Lyons as a food research chemist. Here, she was based in Hammersmith and her work was more satisfying and experimental. She was able to live in Dartford, and take a full part in social life there. This proved life-changing in more ways than one. At a supper party after her adoption meeting, she met Denis Thatcher. He was some ten years older than Margaret Roberts, and a successful and well-off man. They were both avid readers, but Denis introduced Margaret

'Vote Right to Keep What's Left'
'Stop the Rot, Sack the Lot'
1950 ELECTION SLOGANS

Roberts to a wider and more active social life. They went to the theatre, to restaurants, and for drives in his Jaguar. Marriage was on the cards from early on in their relationship, but there were few Saturdays not taken up with either rugby or politics. In the event, the news that he had proposed and she had accepted was released just before the 1950 election.

The 1950 election was hard fought. Deptford was an 'unwinnable' constituency, linked to Chislehurst, Gravesend, and Bexley Heath. Edward Heath stood in Bexley Heath, and the neighbouring associations were expected to support him in his potentially winnable seat. This was the election where Nye Bevan referred to Conservatives as little better than vermin. His comment gave Margaret Roberts and other young Conservatives 'open season' to be rats: they wore little blue rat badges, and established a hierarchy where 'vile vermin' had recruited ten new party members. Thatcher and the Roberts were highly visible. Alfred spoke in the constituency, Muriel worked with the campaign team, and Denis looked after problems and logistics. This is the last time Muriel is mentioned in Margaret Thatcher's memoirs. She married a farmer as he took on the lease of a 300-acre farm. In true Roberts fashion, he bought the farm and increased his holding to 900 acres. The couple farmed succesfully for two decades, staying out of the public eye. When she died, in 2004, they were extremely wealthy. Margaret Roberts herself, at 24, spent her days in a tailored suit from Bourne and Hollingsworth. She used a soapbox in the streets, she attended local markets, she spoke at public meetings almost every night, she replied to every constituency letter, she canvassed inside and outside the factories. She only avoided pubs – Methodism was still against alcohol. This campaign established her as a national figure. As the youngest candidate and as a woman she was always news-worthy. Her public pronouncements were short and sweet – 'Vote Right to Keep What's Left' or 'Stop the Rot, Sack the Lot'. She cut the Labour majority by 6,000.

The end of the election campaign left her tired but exhilarated. It was a well-fought campaign, and the young Margaret Roberts had found a way of life that was exciting and satisfying. It was hard to see how it could be continued. But it was clear that there would be another election very soon – the Labour majority was so reduced the party could not continue in government for long. The hiatus gave her time to move to a small flat in Pimlico, and to learn to drive and acquire her first car. She inherited a pre-war Ford Prefect bought for Muriel for £129 by their father. By the time the second election was called, in October 1951, she and her car were well known in Dartford. She had also had more free time with Denis. She shaved a further 1,000 off the Labour majority, and saw a Conservative government re-elected. She met both Anthony Eden and Churchill while on constituency duties, and kept up her contacts with Conservative Central Office.

This second election marked a period of change in Margaret Roberts' life. In December, she married Denis. The marriage took place in City Road, London, but was celebrated by the Methodist Minister from Grantham. The reception was at the magnificent home of Sir Alfred Bossom, MP for Maidstone. The honeymoon was in Madeira. In the 1950s this was no package holiday. For Margaret Roberts, now Thatcher, it was her first trip out of the country and her first flight on a seaplane. On their return, Margaret Thatcher moved into Denis' sixth-floor flat in Flood Street, Chelsea. This period of her life was *very heaven*.[6] The neighbours were friendly, and often very distinguished. The young couple entertained regularly. Rationing ended and new fruits appeared in the shops. Fashion recovered from wartime austerity, and new clothes could be bought. Coffee bars and restaurants opened. Television entered most houses, though not the Thatchers. The couple attended cinemas and theatres, although 'kitchen sink drama' was never as popular with Margaret Thatcher as *South Pacific*. Ascot, the Derby, Henley and Wimbledon once more became the province of gossip writers – a taste Margaret Thatcher was a little ashamed of. The high spot of this period was the coronation of the new Queen in 1953 – Margaret and Denis bought tickets just opposite Westminster Abbey – a good investment, as it poured with rain all the day and the young couple stayed dry.

The most important change was that she no longer had to earn her living. Marriage to Denis meant that the Lyons' job was no longer necessary. Alfred Roberts' daughter would always expect to earn her own living, but now she had some choice about how that could be done. She had the time and space to consider her next move. As always, it was Alfred Roberts who provided the key. As Mayor of Grantham, he had sat on the bench, and Margaret had accompanied him to court. They had been dined by a King's Council called Norman Winning, who had fascinated her with his discussion of the working of the law. He had studied Physics at Cambridge, and had told her of the possibility of joining the Inns of Court and studying for the bar part time. She had done this in 1950 – now with Denis' support she was able to concentrate on her studies without taking up new employment.

Running a home and studying for the Bar did not take all Margaret Thatcher's time or fulfil her ambitions. She approached Central Office to be considered for another seat, with Denis' full support. At 26, she was far from being 'on the shelf'. Her writing was in demand, and she was an active speaker. However, she was not immediately selected, which was lucky. In August 1953, she gave birth to twin babies, Carol and Mark. At the time, Denis was at the Oval watching a test match. Before the age of mobile phones, he was quite unaware that his wife's pregnancy had culminated in twins delivered by caesarean section – they had only expected one baby. As soon as she was home, Margaret Thatcher paid to take her Bar exams in six months time. Like many new mothers, she hoped that this psychological trick would prevent her from being overwhelmed by the demands of two babies. Unlike many mothers at the time she had the help of a live-in nanny who became a family friend.

When the twins were six months old, Margaret Thatcher had already taken and passed her Bar exams. She wished to specialise in tax law, and so began a journey through different chambers in preparation. She also asked to be put forward for the Orpington constituency – winnable and next to Dartford. She did not get the seat. She was not a candidate in the 1955 election. She was building alliances through the bar networks, and was still in close touch with the party. She was also considered for safe seats at Orpington, Hemel Hempstead and Maidstone, but a young mother with twins was not seen as a safe bet for a safe seat. She was furious about this – she wrote and spoke about the rights of married women to fulfil their potential at work. In 1958, she put herself forward for Finchley, in North London. Here, she paid great attention to her presentation: *I decided to obey instructions and wear the black coat dress. I saw no harm either in courting the fates: so I wore not just my lucky pearls but also a lucky brooch which had been given to me by my Conservative friends in Dartford.*[7]

I saw no harm either in courting the fates: so I wore not just my lucky pearls but also a lucky brooch which had been given to me by my Conservative friends in Dartford.

THATCHER

The constituency party saw a well-off professional woman, well-tailored and well-groomed. Her husband was not with her – he was on a business trip and learned of the selection two days later from the London *Evening Standard*. In 1959, the constituency rewarded the party and her by returning her to Westminster with a big increase in the Conservative majority. Her first task as an MP was to take the six-year-old twins to tea on the terrace of the House of Commons.

The Margaret Thatcher who entered Parliament was a very different woman from the Margaret Roberts who had gone to Oxford. Marriage to Denis had given her social confidence and the freedom to pursue a professional career, but perhaps more importantly it had separated her from Grantham and from Methodism. Her lifestyle now was social and cosmopolitan. The wife of a successful businessman, she had holidayed in Paris and Germany and had entertained and been entertained on a grand scale. She even drank wine. Her own hard work had separated her intellectually. She had read widely, and included works like Hayek's *The Road To Serfdom*, the work that described parliamentary socialism and collectivist policies in general as steps in a route that would lead to a state where individual freedoms were non-existent. It was an influential piece of writing among right-wing thinkers of the time. She had refined and discussed her political opinions with friends in Parliament and at the Bar. Some things had not changed, however – this period of her life confirmed both her dislike and distrust of socialism, and her commitment to economic policies that were practical, sound, and based on 'free-market' principles.

Chapter 3: Taking on the Party

The election on 8 October 1959 saw the Prime Minister Harold Macmillan returned with a majority of 100, and 64 new Conservative MPs. Of these, only Margaret Thatcher had her first taste of office before 1964. She was one of 12 Conservative women (Labour had 13), and younger and better-dressed than her contemporaries. She was slim, attractive, blond, with blue eyes and young children – unusual in the corridors and lobbies of Westminster. She was determined to bring her usual hard work and attention to detail to the new task. She had waited a long time to get to the centre of power – she did not leave Westminster again until her final exit in 1990.

First, she established a 'pair' relationship with an old admirer. Charles Pannell had been leader of Erith Council when Margaret Thatcher had been candidate for Dartford in 1949. Now an established Labour MP, he became her 'pair' – a relationship that continued until his retirement in 1974. The 'pair' relationship, where if one MP is absent the other does not vote, allowed Margaret Thatcher to leave the chamber when necessary. She had a standing date to telephone the twins each night at 6.00 p.m., and her share of parents evenings and constituency duties. She was a fastidious and careful 'pair', and also became good friends with this Labour member – *He was exactly the kind of good-humoured decent Labour man I liked*.[1] For his part, he told fellow Leeds MP Denis Healey to watch her – 'she was exceptionally able, and also a very nice young woman'.[2]

Second, Margaret Thatcher had one stroke of real luck. She was placed third in the regular ballot of backbenchers chosen to present a private member's bill. This annual ballot gives members the opportunity to choose a topic, draft a bill, and speak to it during parliamentary session. The number of bills heard in this way is limited, so candidates pull a number at random from a bag. For Margaret Thatcher, third place gave the opportunity to replace her maiden speech with a memorable introduction of a specific measure.

If the draw was lucky, then the bill was not. Margaret Thatcher had little time to decide, and recognised that this was her opportunity to shine. She was warned against her first choice, a bill changing the law of contempt of court, by the Attorney General with the promise that the government would deal with the matter. In the end, The Public Bodies (Admission of the Press to Meetings) Bill was not a memorable or useful piece of legislation, but steering it through the House showed both determination and skill on Margaret Thatcher's part. It was opposed both because it was seen as an unnecessary measure, designed to upset local authorities that were peaceful in order to discipline the few who were disruptive, and because it was not broad enough – why open up meetings to the press and not to the public as a whole? While Margaret Thatcher agreed that council meetings should be open to the public, she had a specific reason for concentrating on the press. During a recent newspaper dispute, Nottingham and some other Labour councils had denied access to reporters who worked during the strike. This was not a new trick: the Act of 1908 that guaranteed press entry into council meetings could be bypassed if a council went into committee, and the full council could enter committee if it chose. Alfred Roberts had done this in 1937, to avoid reporting of Grantham council overspending. For Margaret Thatcher, the principle was not so much entry into meetings as control of the trade unions and action against strikes. This is the first example of a major theme – control of industrial unrest. She was working in direct agreement with the Conservative manifesto, but against the expressed preference of Henry Brooke, Minister of Housing and Local Government, who wanted a code of conduct rather than a law.

The second reading, at which Margaret Thatcher spoke in defence of her bill, was set down for 5 February. Margaret Thatcher sent 250 hand-written letters to backbench MPs – both Labour and Conservative – to ensure a good turnout. She began without the usual maiden speech conventions of introduction of herself and her constituency: *This is a Maiden Speech, but I know that the constituency of Finchley which I have the honour to represent would not wish me to do other than come straight to the point and address myself to the matter before the house. I cannot do better than begin by stating the object of the Bill ...* [3] She spoke for 27 minutes, clearly and fluently. As a maiden speech by a young, inexperienced and attractive woman it was an unusual feat, and put down a clear marker – Margaret Thatcher had arrived!

She did not speak again for more than a year. She did identify herself by voting in committee for the re-introduction of corporal punishment for young offenders. Drawing perhaps on her experience at the Grantham court with her father, she said: *Some cases which come before the courts concern persons who are so hardened, vicious and amoral that a much more curative element* [than rehabilitation] *is needed in the sentence.* [4] Here again she was out of step with her party, and the amendment was defeated by 26 votes to six. In her final speech as a backbencher she raised a specialised point about powers in relation to speculators: *At present the system of control of Government expenditure is very dangerous in that it gives all the appearance of control without the reality, and that is about the worst situation which one can possibly have.*[5] Another recurring theme of later years.

Her profile both inside and outside Westminster was high during those years on the back benches, even with few parliamentary speeches. Her colleagues, especially those in the Labour Party, seem to have thought highly of her. The veteran Scottish MP Jean Mann wrote of her maiden speech and her family life: 'At this pace, Margaret Thatcher is quite capable of quads and the Foreign Office.'[6] Of course, to expect to be a woman Prime Minister was unthinkable. Legislation giving equal pay and equal rights for women was far in the future. Asked at the Woman of the Year lunch at the Savoy in 1960 who she would like to be, Margaret Thatcher chose Anna Leonowens, the governess at the court of the King of Siam whose story formed the basis for the musical *The King and I.*

'At this pace, Margaret Thatcher is quite capable of quads and the Foreign Office.'

JEAN MANN MP

In 1961, Margaret Thatcher was appointed as Parliamentary Under Secretary (Pensions & National Insurance). This was the year that Mark Thatcher, aged eight, went to boarding school. Carol Thatcher, his twin, went to a different school a year after. Years later, in an interview for the *Daily Telegraph*, she explained: *Mark went because he revels in people all around him and Carol went too, to stop her thinking he was getting preferential treatment.*[7] Carol Thatcher's view, published in her biography of her father, was different. She realised early on, she said, that the best thing she could do for her mother was not to make demands on her time.

Pensions was not a high-profile or glamorous post, but it did give a real grounding in the business of managing government. Later, she sent John Major to the same post saying in her memoirs: *If that did not alert him to the realities of social security and the dependency culture nothing would.*[8] Not much was expected of Margaret Thatcher. Her first Minister, John Boyd Carpenter, came to meet her on the first day, but only because to him she was a lady. His initial expectations were low. She was succeeding a woman, in a post that was perhaps seen as a woman's job. He was frankly scornful. 'I thought quite frankly when Harold Macmillan appointed her that it was just a little bit of a gimmick on his part. Here was a good looking woman and he was obviously, I thought, trying to brighten up the image of his government.'[9]

He was wrong. Margaret Thatcher's tax and chemistry-trained mind made light of learning the intricacies of the system, and her job was, in the main, to refuse change in the laws with as little upheaval as possible. In this she was ferocious, and adept at parliamentary debate. She was not always charming, and had little patience with questioners who had not done exhaustive preparation. She was smart, well turned-out, and hard-working. She was interested in her appearance – opening a Conservative fundraiser in Finchley, she remarked on the pure pleasure of fashion, and that, *You are apt to see the very outfit you are looking for walking down the high street at Finchley.*[10]

She served out this apprenticeship until 1965, in and out of government. She took away from it two enduring lessons. Civil servants, she felt, were by and large uncreative people. Their advice would change, depending on their understanding of what view the minister would take. Secondly, the complicated system of welfare benefits, in the main, contributed to a dependency culture rather than a way of meeting need. This view was not shaken by her attention to detail and to those areas where she felt need was not met sufficiently. For instance, she argued to increase the widowed mothers' allowance, fuelled by the memory of women eking out the household budget by buying bruised fruit in her fathers' shop.

Perhaps her finest hour in the post came in 1962, the day after Macmillan's drastic cull of his Cabinet. The first business of the day was questions to the Minister of Pensions but Boyd Carpenter had been promoted to the Cabinet, and his successor had not been named. The junior ministers faced 15 questions, 14 of which Margaret Thatcher could and did answer clearly and concisely. She displayed a light touch, even humour that lifted Tory spirits. One onlooker commented: 'Amid the gloom and depression of the parliamentary benches she alone radiated confidence, cheerfulness and charm.'[11] In a demoralised Tory party, this was a small bright moment.

But the Macmillan era was coming to an end. Margaret Thatcher had little say in the leadership question, Douglas-Home succeeded an ailing Prime Minister and led the party into the 1964 election. She liked Douglas-Home: he had come to speak when she was President of the Oxford University Conservative Association, and she found him easy to talk to. Her feelings on the great issues of the government were well known, and likely to be in line with the new leader: she believed in co-operation and rapport with the United States, and where possible with Russia; she supported entry into the European Common Market as a trade treaty. At the Conservative Party AGM in March 1962 she put a questionnaire on each seat, asking how members would solve the problems of the day. Her speech started by praising the development of Britain. *We have what Americans have described as an affluent society. We have had a tremendous increase in material benefits over the last few years. If Karl Marx were to come back here, he would surely not be able to say 'Workers you have nothing to lose but your lives', but instead 'you have nothing to lose but your refrigerator, your car, your TV, and all your other luxuries'.*[12] And she went on to show, with figures and statistics, that British workers could not continue to pay themselves more than they earned and that Britain must not be out of step with overseas competitors. She defended Selwyn Lloyd's pay pause, while identifying herself with mounting backbench pressure to curb industrial action. She campaigned valiantly for Finchley during the election, and was rewarded by being returned with a majority reduced only to 9,000. The young, energetic Labour leader Harold Wilson formed a government with a parliamentary majority of four, and for Margaret Thatcher the shadow backbench years began. Alec Douglas-Home resigned shortly after the election. His lasting legacy was the system of election that brought a very different leader to the party. The candidates, Reginald Maudling, Enoch Powell and Edward Heath, were all important characters in the life of Margaret Thatcher. She voted for Edward Heath, with whom she had shared platforms during the Dartford

Ted has a passion to get Britain right and of course, so did Keith, and so did I.

THATCHER

campaigns. She says it was Keith Joseph who influenced her choice. As far as he was concerned; *Ted has a passion to get Britain right and of course, so did Keith, and so did I.*[13] When Wilson called a snap election in March 1966 Margaret Thatcher campaigned wholeheartedly for Heath. *I stand for a Conservative Government because I believe that the State was made for Man and not Man for the State. That ability and hard work should be encouraged by taxation incentives. That freedom of choice in schools, goods and services should continue and increase. That we should take the initiative in foreign affairs and not merely follow our American friends. That in Edward Heath we have a man of*

ACTION, INTEGRITY and PURPOSE – a fitting leader for a great nation.[14] She held Finchley, even increasing her majority to 9,464, but Wilson was returned as Prime Minister with a majority of 98.

After the election, Margaret Thatcher had been moved from Pensions. First, she went to Housing and Land, to oppose Labour moves to establish the Land Commission, a means of nationalising the gains made by redevelopment. Here she became aware of anomalies in the rating system – her first conference speech was about reform of household rates. From there, she became Treasury spokesperson on Tax under Iain Macleod. But this was not a good time for her. Denis, so long the mainstay of her parliamentary career, was facing business problems. The family firm was becoming less profitable. The obvious choice was to sell to a bigger multinational firm, but he was reluctant to take that step. Tired and concerned, he went to South Africa immediately after the election for some time to think and regroup. When he returned, he sold the family firm. His money enabled Margaret Thatcher's career, but that meant Denis had to continue earning the money: not only Margaret Thatcher, but the twins with their expensive school fees, his mother, and other relatives relied on his finances. In practice, the sale of the family business safeguarded the family income and made Denis a millionaire, but that was not foreseeable in 1964. Also Margaret Thatcher herself was tired and depressed by the election defeat. At the end of the year she became ill, for almost the first time in her adult life.

Yet promotion came quickly in the small parliamentary party. Between 1964 and 1970 she held six different port-folios – three as a junior spokeswoman (Pensions, Housing, Economic Policy) and three as a member of the shadow cabinet, shadowing power, transport and education. Her approach to economic policy was indicative of her approach to all roles: In preparing herself for her first Commons speech opposing Callaghan's Budget she took from the House of Commons library every Budget speech and Finance Bill since the war and read them. *I was thus able to demonstrate to a somewhat bemused Jim Callaghan ... that this was the only budget which had failed to make even a minor concession in the social services area.*[15]

She threw herself into her home life, as well. With both children at boarding school, the Thatcher's rented a small flat a stone's-throw from the Houses of Parliament. For family weekends and holidays they bought a mock-Tudor house near Tunbridge Wells. One of Margaret Thatcher's hobbies was interior decorating – she renovated and designed each room over their time in the house. She painted and papered the eight bedrooms herself, but called in professional help to do the staircase and hall. She had collected good mahogany furniture and silverware – perhaps reminiscent of the dark wood of her father's shops. She had space to make a garden – her efforts in previous homes had been small-scale. Here she could make the sort of garden she loved. *Oh yes, I love gardening but not the sort of formal display gardening so much but really creating a garden of shrubs and with if possible just a little bit of woodland at the bottom of the garden with bluebells and primroses and things in. But then you do need to use some annuals to get some colour for the time of year when you can't otherwise and I've been lucky to have gardens with acid soil and I love creating the rhododendrons, azalea, heather garden.*[16] The house was not used as much as she hoped, however. The twins preferred to spend time in London, and both Margaret and Denis Thatcher worked long hours. The flat was much more convenient.

By 1972 Margaret Thatcher's fortunes had changed again. The 1970 election saw the Conservative Party again in power with a majority of 31. More important, it saw Margaret

Thatcher returned to become Secretary of State for Education and Science. Alfred Roberts was not there to see it – he had died in February. This was a different, more cosmopolitan Margaret Thatcher. In 1967 she visited the United States, was taken into American hearts and homes and shown the benefits of that free trade democracy, including the space centre where in the future men would leave to stand on the moon. Two years later, she visited Russia, and saw how *behind the official propaganda, the grey streets, all but empty shops and badly maintained workers' housing blocks, Russian humanity peeped out.*[17]

Behind the official propaganda, the grey streets, all but empty shops and badly maintained workers' housing blocks, Russian humanity peeped out.

THATCHER

She bought a porcelain tea service, the pride of her growing china collection. In her memoirs, she said it always reminded her with pain of the sight of working mothers taking their children to nursery at 6.30 in the morning, to leave them all day. Her children were still at boarding schools, allowing her time for travel and her career.

In 1965, Rhodesia had declared unilateral independence from Britain, which had imposed sanctions. The British army was now deployed in Belfast, and in 1968 the Soviet army had invaded Czechoslovakia. Business was still growing, but immigration figures had been rising steadily and sterling had been devalued. Nearer home, this government had been elected on a manifesto finally polished at a Shadow Cabinet conference in Selsdon, at which Margaret Thatcher took a full part. The manifesto was neither new nor the absolute swing to the right it was portrayed as being. It was a set of coherent policies, forged over the years in opposition. It allowed the new government to enter office with clear direction.

For Margaret Thatcher, hitting the ground running meant

entering her ministry with a list scribbled in an exercise book of things to be addressed that day. Some were small administrative matters, but the big issue addressed equality in education and comprehensive schools, a constant issue in educational policy since 1945. There is common agreement that compulsory education is an enormous force for social change, and that force can be used to ensure equality among children, but there is no political agreement about how equality should be reached, or even what equality is. The poles of the argument are on one hand that children should all be educated together, with no distinction of money, parentage, or ability. This will encourage children to find their own level, and ensure that structural inequalities become a thing of the past. This way of thinking about education lead to big comprehensive secondary schools, the end of school selection by ability, and moves to end the 11-Plus. On the other hand, the argument is that children should be given the opportunity and the incentive to succeed, therefore selection at 11 should be retained. This will allow successful, hard-working children or children of successful parents to benefit and to develop their academic ability, while other children benefit from smaller groups and more vocational teaching. Margaret Thatcher's position was clear. She had already told the press that she would withdraw Tony Crosland's Circular 10/65 under which local authorities were required to submit plans for re-organising secondary education on comprehensive lines, and Circular 10/66, which withheld capital funding from local education authorities that refused to go comprehensive. This was her first battle with her officials. In order to withdraw a circular, another command paper had to be written. Should this new command paper not include a detailed outline of potential educational systems to replace comprehensive schooling? Margaret Thatcher thought not. Not only could that take a lot of time, it was also not the role of government to dictate education policy to local authorities. Circular 10/70 was issued on Tuesday 30 June 1970. This was an absolute coup for the party and its supporters, but less successful as policy. All local education plans for comprehensive schools had to be signed by the Secretary of State for Education. Margaret Thatcher, during her time in that role, signed more plans for comprehensive schools and the subsequent closure of grammar schools than any Education Secretary before or since.

The dislike that the Department felt for her was deep-rooted, and she felt that she was not among friends. She saw the Department and the teaching unions as closely linked, and committed to comprehensive education. She was not a philosophical heavy-weight, and preferred musicals to opera. She saw the process of education not as entry into a world of learning, but as the learning of a body of knowledge. She had taught for six weeks in her first Oxford summer vacation – maths and science at Grantham boys' school – and prized herself on having 'gone on' until the boys got it and not having let them go until they'd got it. This approach did not sit well with idealistic images of developing a new society through education. But she was very soon personally popular with the staff. She would always make someone coffee, or

> The 11-Plus was an examination based on intelligence testing, designed to channel children at the age of 11 into appropriate schooling – grammar schools for academically-able children, secondary modern schools for more vocational training. Although success in the exam could be the route out of poverty, failure could see a child condemned to a second-class education. The system has been widely criticised as being culturally and class biased, and for perpetuating inequality. The debate about selective versus comprehensive schools continues unabated to this day.

find time to talk or sign a 'get well' card. And she was a heavyweight fighter when it came to protecting the Department's budget. She also showed herself able to step outside budget restraints and set her own priorities. For example, as she entered office, the Open University had been doomed to closure by Iain Macleod. He had been firm about ending the 'great socialist opportunity for the part-time student to graduate'.[18] Margaret Thatcher, however, driven by her strong belief in giving opportunities to those who worked hard, was equally firm about keeping it open.

Margaret Thatcher was Secretary of State for Education for three years and eight months. She had made seven points during the election campaign:

- A shift of emphasis onto primary schools – carried out with the help of a comprehensive programme of building.
- Expansion of nursery education.
- The right of local education authorities to decide what secondary scheme was best for their area, while defending and retaining the best of traditional schools.
- Raising the age of school leaving to 16.
- Encouraging direct-grant schools and retaining private schools.
- Expanding further and higher education.
- Holding an inquiry into teacher training.

And these were her priorities in office. It was these priorities, and increasing pressure to make budget cuts, that led to her becoming 'Maggie Thatcher the Milk Snatcher' in November 1971 – a demon to the press and public. She implemented another of Iain Macleod's decisions – to remove free milk from primary school children. The resulting outcry is, in retrospect, surprising. The previous Labour government had already cut free milk to secondary-school children, and Margaret Thatcher's saving promised £8 million to build primary schools. Perhaps it was the increasing austerity of the Conservative government, dogged by inflation. Free milk had been one of the reasons that poor children grew up in better health in the 1970s than they did in the 1930s and 1940s, but other changes in housing and welfare had also improved health. Taking away free milk was a direct attack on the prevailing ideas of the time, that the government was responsible for welfare, but the publicity did not stress this. It is hard not to see some of the outcry as being aimed at a woman in Parliament, and a well-heeled, well-dressed Tory woman to boot. Later, during the leadership campaign, she sparked a similar storm about hoarding food by saying, *Well, you call it stockpiling, I call it being a prudent housewife and the kind of life I've led you have to buy things when food was comparatively cheap – you know you bought the fruit in summer, you made it into jam, you packed it into kilner jars, you put it on your shelves. Most country women or people brought up in small towns did this as a matter of prudent housewifery… . Of course housewives are in fact doing this. How do you think that … it is that the deep freeze sales are going so well, that frozen food centres have sprung up all over the country? This is what people are doing, they are prudently putting aside money to put things into deep freezes. My point is a perfectly simple one: if you buy it in tins you don't have to pay or use electricity in which to store things.*[19] This led to a series of headlines and adverse comments. On both occasions her innocence and ignorance about life as it was lived in industrial Britain led her to appear as the consummate Tory lady.

Well, you call it stockpiling, I call it being a prudent housewife and the kind of life I've led you have to buy things when food was comparatively cheap.

THATCHER

Her life as Denis Thatcher's wife contributed to the image, but the decisions were pure Alfred Roberts' economics, and the priorities of the Grantham middle classes.

While Margaret Thatcher was working towards her priorities in education, the Heath government was in increasing trouble. Their mandate had been based on a programme to regenerate the economy. They wanted to reduce government support for industry, but in 1971 they nationalised Rolls Royce. Margaret Thatcher was broadly in favour despite her antipathy towards nationalisation: here, defence needs took priority. By 1972 though, the government had passed a statute taking legal powers to control all increases in pay, prices and dividends. This U-turn, in Margaret Thatcher's eyes, was unforgivable, although none of her public statements in 1972 would have given that impression. In her memoirs she identifies three events which *together tried the Government's resolve and found it wanting*:[20] the miners' strike, the financial problems of Upper Clyde Shipbuilders and the unemployment total reaching one million. The miners' strike ended when Heath conceded to the miners' demands, but the price was increasing wage control. To Margaret Thatcher this was 'Danegeld', a ransom forced on the country because the government had not been well enough prepared to withstand industrial unrest. The Clyde shipbuilders had their subsidy restored. Unemployment, in Margaret Thatcher's view, was a direct result of Roy Jenkins' tight fiscal policies of 1969–70, and would soon peak and begin to fall. But the Heath government was a collective. When the full story of this cabinet is released it will be clearer to what extent Margaret Thatcher argued. What is known is that Edward Heath called a snap general election in February 1974. The Yom Kippur War the previous October had raised oil prices. The coal miners were on strike, and without oil or coal Britain was working on power for only three days a week. People were cold, the days were dark. Shops were lighted by candles and gas lights, industry was shutting down. Heath called the election to get a public mandate to deal firmly with the miners, but with only three weeks for campaigning this election was disastrous for the Conservatives.

No party was returned with an overall majority. The ambiguous situation made it legitimate for Heath to stay in office, and try to form a coalition with the Liberals. Margaret Thatcher vehemently opposed this, saying publicly that her policies would not be transferred to a 'National Government'. The attempt failed as it was bound to do: even a Liberal/ Conservative pact would not have given an overall majority. Heath resigned in March, and Harold Wilson formed his second administration. It was clear this would not last long – in October a second election returned Wilson but with an overall majority of only three.

Edward Heath did not resign as leader of the party. He had now lost three elections out of four, but he did not fall on his sword. On 14 October, the backbench 1922 Committee conveyed their opinion to Heath: that unless he stood down there must be a fresh election. Heath refused to discuss it until after the 1922 executive elections. On 14 November, he agreed to an election after the Committee had revised the rules. The first ballot was held on 4 February 1975. If Heath had resigned at this point, the most likely successor was Willie Whitelaw who had refused to stand against Heath, but Heath refused to stand down. Likely opponents from the right, supported by Margaret Thatcher, were Edward Du Cann and Keith Joseph. Du Cann did not stand for personal reasons. Joseph made it clear that he would stand for the right of the party when the opportunity arose, but, like Whitelaw, the centre and left of the party were bound by loyalty to Heath. Margaret Thatcher supported Joseph. Not only his friend, she also believed in his economic and social portfolio – market freedom. When the Conservatives had lost the second election, and a leadership contest became inevitable, she crossed herself off the list of candidates in order to make space for Joseph. Keith Joseph himself sabotaged his chances. During that summer he had planned to make three speeches outlining the mistakes of the last 30 years and describing the way forward. The third of these, in October at Edgbaston, included references to social class and comments on birth control that seemed to revive issues of eugenics. The uproar following this made it clear to him that he would be unelectable as leader. On the day that he withdrew from the contest, Margaret Thatcher announced her candidacy.

She was now shadowing the Secretary of State for the Environment. Her task was high-profile – to establish a manifesto commitment that would appeal to voters, would not be seen to criticise previous Conservative policy, and was recognisably 'conservative'. For the first time the 'right to buy' for council tenants became part of an election commitment. Despite the looming leadership contest, Margaret Thatcher enjoyed these months. In November, she had been moved to shadow the Treasury. Opposing Labour economic policy found her in her element, and the approaching leadership contest allowed her to hone her campaigning skills. Airey Neave ran her campaign. He was a right-wing Conservative MP who had quarrelled with Heath early in his career. He was also a likeable man with a distinguished war record. Margaret Thatcher came to prize his political support and friendship. He encouraged her to concentrate on the Finance Bill. That way, MPs had the opportunity to see her in action. She would address her core supporters in a committee room at the house from 10.30 p.m. until midnight – afterwards she commented on how good it had felt to talk about things she believed in. She emphasised her *conservativeness*: that she stood for sound economics, middle-class values, ordinary British people. She wrote a letter to her constituency party focusing on the need to listen to ordinary human beings with ordinary human needs. On 4 February Margaret Thatcher defeated Edward Heath in the first ballot for Tory leader. Heath resigned. There was, of course, a second ballot: Margaret Thatcher's majority had not been sufficient to avoid that. Now Heath's allies were free to stand, and Jim Prior, John Peyton and Geoffrey Howe did. Only Howe had any right-wing credentials. On 11 February 1975 Margaret Thatcher was elected leader of the Conservative Party – Leader of the Opposition.

Chapter 4: Thatcher Emerging

The first hours of leadership were a round of engagements. First to meet the press at Westminster Hall, then to Central Office to be greeted by the staff. Denis was at Bill Sheldon's house in Pimlico for a celebration with friends. Margaret Thatcher had tried to reach him with the news, but the press got there first. Mark learned the news at work, while Carol had to wait until her solicitor's exam finished. It was late at night before all the family could be together. Margaret Thatcher had kept to a routine with her family: breakfast and as much of the weekend as possible together. Now the twins were grown up, and life would never be the same again.

The morning of 12 February dawned as something of an anti-climax. Margaret Thatcher was now the first woman leader of a major political party in the West, and had won her leadership election fair and square. But she was leader of a deeply-divided party, and she had divided it. Her support came from the backbenchers not from the Shadow Cabinet, who had been loyal to Heath until the end. Nor was Edward Heath going to help heal this division. She called at his home to honour her commitment to invite him into the Shadow Cabinet, but he refused. It was a quick meeting – Heath's personal private secretary detained her before she left so that the waiting press would not realise how quick. During the following year and at the party conference he ignored any attempt at reconciliation. This behaviour ensured that Shadow Cabinet members who might have gathered behind him to oppose her had no focus. Heath became an outsider within the party.

Traditionally, the Conservative Party rallies to a new leader, and this leader was both in the public eye and possibly more vulnerable because she was a woman. Key elders of the party, Alec Douglas-Home, Lord Hailsham and Peter Carrington, set an example in supporting her. Willie Whitelaw, her nearest rival in the leadership contest, became a loyal deputy. He put aside his own ambitions to lead the party, accepting that at his age the chance would not come again. He is said to have announced her leadership, and his acceptance of defeat, in the same speech and in floods of tears at a dinner that night. He had nothing in common, personally, socially or politically with Mrs Thatcher the grocer's daughter and found her abruptness and single-mindedness distressing. Nevertheless, he was a conscientious and supportive colleague until his retirement. His support made a great deal of difference in the next years.

Her Shadow Cabinet appointments were designed to reassure. Two members of the existing cabinet stepped down in solidarity with Heath. Robert Carr and Peter Walker were returned to the back benches – although she had got on well with Peter Walker, he was an outspoken critic of Keith Joseph's right-wing policies and so needed to go. Keith Joseph himself was appointed as her private economic advisor with responsibility for policy and research. The remaining members of the Shadow Cabinet stayed. They were joined by Geoffrey Howe as Shadow Chancellor. Of five new faces only one was a woman, Sally Oppenheim, who took the classic woman's portfolio of consumer affairs. One was Airey Neave, the only appointment that went to an outright supporter. He was given the post he wanted, Northern Ireland.

The composition of the Shadow Cabinet was a reaction to the circumstances of her leadership, and preceded a struggle for the direction of the party that was to continue during the next four years in opposition. These were tiring and frustrating years for an inexperienced leader. Margaret Thatcher was becoming more and more convinced by right-wing monetarist policies, but in practice, it was clear that the party had to rebuild relationships with the trade unions, and had to retain some 'middle ground' credibility. The debate inside the Tory party, and outside in wider society, reflected a change in British politics that went further than ideas about Tories as necessarily right-wing and well-heeled and Labour as being on the side of the workers, into fundamental understandings of freedom and equality.

When Clement Attlee was elected Prime Minister in 1945, he said 'I will not cease from mental strife, nor shall my sword sleep in my hand, 'Till we have built Jerusalem in England's Green and Pleasant Land.' Margaret Thatcher could have used exactly the same lines, but would have meant a very different Jerusalem. To Attlee, and to succeeding governments after the war, the dream was of a land where each and every individual was equal in the eyes of the government: where there was full employment, and where the state was responsible for the welfare and education of the people. To make this happen, economic theory drew on the work of John Maynard Keynes. Keynesian economic ideas meant that the government supported manufacturing industry either by providing subsidies or by taking control into their own hands through nationalisation. Subsidised or nationalised industries could support wage rises, so that workers could afford to buy the goods made. Keynes believed that this process would form a 'virtuous circle', where the amount gained from selling goods was always increasing, and therefore more people could buy goods and more people would be involved in the manufacturing process. The government would be able to support the circle through taxation, and would be responsible for using that taxation to support welfare – including full employment. In this ever-growing economy the government would also provide education and health services that gave free entry to everybody, and so minimised inequalities of class and wealth. In this way, people would be freed from anxiety, fear and the need to compete, and would create a free-thinking, well-educated, hard-working society supporting each other and the government.

These ideas had been tested by changes in British society in the post-war years. World events had altered the economic climate in which governments operated. For instance, the pace of post-war reconstruction had been slowed by the need for American finance through the Marshall Plan, and later industrial expansion had been slowed by the rising price of oil. Britain's ability to market its goods was threatened by cheaper alternatives made in the Far East. The population was increased by immigrant workers. Reports of life in communist Russia did not inspire confidence in socialism, while American images of free enterprise were exciting. The long-running debate about entry into the Common Market changed the climate in which the Keynesian closed circle could operate. But the biggest challenge came from home. Margaret Thatcher had already warned that Britain was paying itself more than it earned: Throughout the Heath government union pressure for increases in wages was expressed through strikes and unrest. Agreement between governments and workers, without which the Keynesian circle could not function, was breaking down.

Despite the pressure on Keynesian economic measures, prime ministers from Attlee to Wilson had accepted, to a greater or lesser extent, the need for government to be involved in industry, wages and prices. This 'collectivist' consensus, supporting bargaining through unions and collective responsibility between workers and government, was perhaps the legacy of the landslide Labour victory in 1945. That had been a vote for a new and different way of arranging society, and equality was fundamental. It was deeply embedded in British thinking. Politically, there was still no real ideological challenge to this basic principle.

Collectivism or Keynesian were not ideologies or principles that Margaret Thatcher agreed with. Her childhood ethic of hard work and success may have given her grounding in individualism. Certainly Alfred Roberts helped others, but he did not do so by losing or threatening his own position. 'Charity begins at home' ensures that what is given is only given after individual and family needs are well catered for. Personally, she was well suited to ideologies that stressed individual gains and individual work. Her first action as Secretary for Education had been to try and slow down the growth of large comprehensive schools. She had a deep distrust of socialists, started by her reading of Hayek at Oxford, made personal by the defeat of her father by socialists in Grantham in 1952, and supported by her visit to Soviet Russia. Her personal views had little outlet in previous years: although Robert Blake

Harold Macmillan had announced the first application for Britain to join the EEC in 1961, but this attempt was vetoed by the French President General de Gaulle in 1963. Edward Heath was intimately involved in Britain's negotiations for membership. In 1971, the House of Commons voted in favour of membership, and Britain joined in 1973. Membership had been confirmed in a referendum called by the Wilson government in 1975. Controversies over Europe were to plague the Conservative Party in the 1990s under Major.

describes the Heath manifesto of 1970 as a 'right wing' document,[1] the actions of the government in office were to continue to support industry and to bargain, where possible, with the unions.

The ideological argument against collectivism was first put forward by Keith Joseph. He spoke about the 'socialist danger' of previous governments, including Conservative ones. These ideas were far more in tune with Margaret Thatcher's instincts, where individual equality and freedom depended not on the actions of the government but in the hard work and enterprise of the individual; where full employment was not a goal but an evil, because it took away the incentive to work hard; where rights to education and housing took away a man's basic duty to care for himself and his own family; and where the taxation and government spending needed to support welfare arrangements was money the individual should have the right to spend themselves. This alternative drew on the economic ideas of Milton Friedman, and became known as 'monetarism'. Here, inflation is seen as happening because the government allows the supply of money in the economy to grow by providing subsidies for industry and wage rises. A government's sole responsibility is to reduce the amount of money in the economy by reducing spending. This action, coupled with valuing individual enterprise and avoiding any form of collectivism, is the foundation of the philosophy that Keith Joseph was speaking about, Margaret Thatcher implemented and which became known as 'Thatcherism'.

On that morning in 1975, these ideas were new and unpopular. Keith Joseph had begun to move away from collectivism during his time in Heath's Cabinet, and had been roundly criticised for it. Most of the members of the re-appointed Shadow Cabinet had supported the collectivist policies of the Heath government, and mistrusted both

Joseph and Margaret Thatcher. Very few of the new appointments were convinced by monetarist ideas. Indeed, very few of the party as a whole were monetarists – links between traditional right-wing Conservative individualism and Friedman's economics were neither tried, tested nor accepted. Throughout the following years, this limited the pool from which new Shadow Cabinet members could be selected.

Margaret Thatcher set out to win hearts and minds. The Tory conference was in October, which gave her seven months to establish a hold, though maybe a tenuous one, on her leadership. These were momentous times in the country. The battle for the European Union was raging – February 1975 saw the country vote to remain in the union in a referendum. In July the government brought forward a pay policy. Margaret Thatcher did not shine in debate against Wilson, and was hampered because by no means all the Tory Party or Shadow Cabinet would accept her speaking her true beliefs on this – that pay policies were fundamentally wrong, and helped cause rather than cure rising inflation. In September, she left for a two-week visit to the USA and Canada, but she was back in time for her first Tory conference as leader.

Her conference speech was a critical test. She did not want to make a speech just about economic policy, she wanted to set the foundations of a real philosophical and practical alternative to collectivist thinking. This was absolutely new ground in a mainstream political forum. Monetarist forerunners like Keith Joseph and Enoch Powell had been cast as mavericks, and the message had been lost in reaction to them personally or to other parts of their speeches.

The process of writing this speech was typical of Margaret Thatcher's style. The first draft came from the Tory party research department. She re-wrote this herself, in her own handwriting. Then it went to Woodrow Wyatt to look at from a journalist's perspective, and had some more material added by the research department. During the week before conference, it passed through many hands, but by the Wednesday it was, according to Margaret Thatcher, *clear to me that none of those working away in my suite was what in the jargon is known as 'wordsmith'. We had the structure, the ideas and even the foundations for some good jokes, but we needed someone with a feel for the words* themselves *who could make the whole text flow along.*[2]

Who could do that effectively? A playwright of course. Ronnie Millar was a successful playwright, with a new play in rehearsal. He endeared himself immediately to Margaret Thatcher – he included some lines from Abraham Lincoln

> 'You cannot strengthen the weak by weakening the strong
> You cannot bring about prosperity by discouraging thrift.
> You cannot help the wage-earner by pulling down the wage-payer.'[3]

Lines that she had already found and kept on a scrap of paper in her handbag. For the next 15 years no major speech was complete until it had been 'Ronnified' – until Ronnie Millar had used his playwright's ability to speak in her voice, and make that voice audible.

This speech was finished at 4.30 in the morning on Friday, and delivered on Saturday. It contained a passage that Margaret Thatcher describes as her 'credo' and quotes in full in her memoirs: *Let me give you my vision: A man's right to work as he will, to spend what he earns, to own property, to have the state as servant and not as master – these are the British inheritance ... We must get private enterprise back on the road to recovery – not merely to give people more of their own money to spend as they choose,*

*but to have more money to help the old and the sick and the handi-
capped ... I believe that, just as each of us has an obligation to make
the best of his talents, so governments have an obligation to create the
framework within which we can do so ... We can go on as we have
been doing, we can continue down. Or we can stand up and with a
decisive act of will we can say 'Enough'.*[4]

It went down very well indeed. The audience loved it.
The press reported it joyfully. *Now I* am *Leader*, she told her
immediate supporters.[5] Millar saw another side of her, though.
He found her looking tired and drawn. This speech had been
alright, but what about the next one? Was this going to be
the best she could do? This was too much for Denis. 'My
God woman, you've just had a bloody great triumph and here
you are worrying yourself sick about next year! I'll get the
others, shall I? Then you can settle down for another all night
session. I mean, obviously there's no time to be lost ... '[6]

This was the year that Denis Thatcher retired from the
management of Burmah Oil, the company that had bought
the family firm and where he had become director, at great
profit to himself. While he did not retire from all his business
interests – his active direc-
torship of other companies
topped up the family's by
now considerable fortune
– he was available to support
Mrs. Thatcher throughout the
trying years in opposition and
in government. The children were grown up. The Thatchers
spent the week at their flat in Flood Street, and the weekends
in the Dower Flat at Scotney Castle at Lambourne that had
replaced the large and underused house. Like most working
women, Margaret Thatcher still had domestic responsibilities, but as the partner of a rich man, these were light.

*We can go on as we have been doing, we
can continue down. Or we can stand up
and with a decisive act of will we can say
'Enough'.*

THATCHER

Denis Thatcher was possibly even more of an individualist Tory than she was herself, with extensive business interests, knowledge and contacts, who had reached a stage where his time could be used flexibly to support his wife. His support was both public and private. If he felt a speech was going badly, he would sit at the back of the hall and clap and shout his agreement. Usually others would follow suit and the tone of the meeting would be changed. He would collect his wife from meetings or conferences that were continuing late, tapping his watch and saying 'Margaret, time for Bedfordshire'.[7] He was the closest advisor Margaret Thatcher ever had, or who she would listen to – constantly beside her in the years to come.

During the next years, she needed his support. She had not only to convince the world and her party that a woman could lead a major Western democracy, she also had to develop and make convincing a whole new ideological perspective on practical policy-making. As she was no match for Harold Wilson in parliamentary debate, she had to look for other ways to make her presence known. She approached the task with typical Thatcher decision and precision. She began with herself. Margaret Roberts had been a successful middle-class girl, earning her place through hard work. Margaret Thatcher must appear to have her place by right and ability. She started with her voice – like many women she had to talk loudly in order to make herself heard in male-dominated political debate, and simply raising the volume had made her sound shrill. This, and the last remnants of her Lincolnshire accent, were taken to a voice coach, and even to the actor Laurence Olivier for advice. The result was a slower, more enunciated and more resonant delivery, reminiscent of the kind of dignified pre-war woman teachers she would remember well. Her hair changed, not only because she had little time and soft, thick hair but also because she had a personal assistant available at all times with heated rollers. Her dress sense began to take account of camera angles and the need to make a strong personal statement. She was fully conscious of the effect of her appearance. Christened the 'Iron Lady' by the official Soviet news agency Tass, after her attacks on defence cuts she said: *Ladies and Gentlemen, I stand before you tonight in my green chiffon evening gown, my face softly made up, my fair hair gently waved ... The Iron Lady of the Western World.*[8] She used the sobriquet often in the future – the contrast between the image and her toughness was useful.

Care of her image went hand in hand with selling the message to the country, through personal appearances and newspaper articles. She was guided by Gordon Reece, part of her full-time staff and an ex-television producer. He could jolly her along to accept things she would otherwise have rejected. He thought that the message should be put to all the electorate, not just readers of heavyweight papers. He even argued that traditionally Labour newspapers like the *Sun* and the *News of the World* would report new ideas, if only to argue against them. This was revolutionary thinking – no leader of either party had set out to woo the press to get a political philosophy in front of all voters. And this was a personal wooing: *he* [Reece] *also persuaded me that the person they really wanted to see and hear from was me. So, whatever the other demands on my diary, when*

The 'Iron Lady' was not the only nickname Margaret Thatcher acquired in her career. The Liberal MP and broadcaster Clement Freud christened her 'Attila the Hen', her colleague Norman St John Stevas called her 'The Immaculate Misconception' and the Conservative MP Julian Critchley once referred to her as 'The Great She-Elephant', somewhat to the displeasure of his constituency association.

Gordon said that we must have lunch with such-and-such an editor, that was the priority.[9]

It is unlikely that she needed much persuasion. To her, changing political course was a mission bordering on a religion. It was not only a practical answer to Britain's problems, it was also a way to defend people from the harm that socialism did to their lives, their prospects and their characters. To Margaret Thatcher, the trade unions were quickly becoming the best possible example of the damage socialism could do. How the unions would deal with the Conservatives after Edward Heath's defeat at their hands was at the centre of party policy-making over the next years. In 1976, Margaret Thatcher reshuffled her Shadow Cabinet. John Biffen joined – a strong critic of Heath's corporatist approach. Douglas Hurd, one of Heath's closest aides, became party spokesman on Europe. Willie Whitelaw became Shadow Home Secretary, and Ian Gilmour moved to defence. This was still not a purely monetarist and individualist group, but it did allow Keith Joseph, still head of research and policy, Geoffrey Howe, Jim Prior and Margaret Thatcher to approach the Confederation of British Industry (CBI) to discuss possible futures. The result horrified her: *These men were managers who had lost all hope of ever really managing their companies again.*[10] While she could not accept such defeatism, the experience did convince her that she must show herself able to work with trade unions. Accordingly, she told the Young Conservatives in early February that *it would not be difficult to work with responsible trade union leadership.* She did not specify what she might see as responsible leadership.

She was less circumspect in discussion of defence policy. She saw Soviet communism as an ideological and a practical threat. In Kensington in January, she made this crystal-clear: *No. The Russians are bent on world dominance, and they are rapidly acquiring the means to become the most powerful imperial nation the world has ever seen. The men in the Soviet Politburo do not have to worry about the ebb and flow of public opinion. They put guns before butter, while we put just about everything before guns. They know that they are a super power in only one sense – the military sense. They are a failure in human and economic terms.*[11] This open criticism of another power and of government defence policy was breathtakingly undiplomatic, but popular in the country: her personal popularity rating shot up by seven points. Her call for strong defence and her scepticism of government foreign policy was finally too much for Reginald Maudling, the Shadow Foreign and Commonwealth Secretary. He complained that Margaret Thatcher had unilaterally committed the Shadow Cabinet to massive re-armament. He lost his post a few weeks later. But in truth Margaret Thatcher was not taking her personal policies from the Shadow Cabinet. As she saw it, she was still a trailblazer slowly establishing a following rather than a spokesperson for a united front. The real debate in the Shadow Cabinet was leading to the publication of *The Right Approach* in October 1976, the first Conservative publication to begin to lay down the practical alternatives to socialism.

Meanwhile, the Labour majority in Parliament was shrinking. In March 1976, Harold Wilson resigned and was replaced by Jim Callaghan. She was no more successful in the House against Callaghan than she had been against Wilson, appearing nervous and gauche in the face of his huge experience. But within weeks he gave her the opportunity to cause real trouble. There was a close-run vote on the devolution of Scotland, which the government might lose. Many MPs had pairing arrangements and therefore were not voting, but the government would be one vote short at the crucial lobby. Government whips seized a reluctant Labour pair, and pushed him through the voting lobby. This would have been a bad breach of parliamentary etiquette at any time, but the vote won by the single disputed vote nationalised the aircraft and shipbuilding industries. The Conservatives immediately called off pairing and all other business arrangements with the government. Callaghan was forced to re-run the vote, but now it was an outright victory and nationalisation continued.

The state of the economy was worsening. The sterling crises of 1976 forced the government to impose spending cuts that Margaret Thatcher had to support, and gave Callaghan the chance to remind electors that Margaret Thatcher and Keith Joseph had been high spenders in Heath's government. By March 1977 only a Liberal/Labour pact kept Callaghan in government. It was becoming a real possibility that the Conservative Party would be in power and Margaret Thatcher would be Prime Minister. The party conference in September would be a crucial test of her leadership, and economic policy still divided the Shadow Cabinet. The paper before the conference was *the right approach to the economy* – she described it as a rather *unhappy compromise document*.[12] The conference passed without major incident, but the issue of how to deal with the unions did not go away. Geoffrey Howe made a speech in January 1978 attacking the role of trade unions in Britain, but without Shadow Cabinet

The counterpart of the withdrawal of government from interference in prices and profits in the private sector which both we and you want to see, is inevitably the withdrawal of government from interference in wage bargaining. There can be no selective return to personal responsibility.

THATCHER

endorsement. Margaret Thatcher made a much less precise attack a few days later, saying: *The counterpart of the withdrawal of government from interference in prices and profits in the private sector which both we and you want to see, is inevitably the withdrawal of government from interference in wage bargaining. There can be no selective return to personal responsibility.*[13] The speech was made to Scottish industrialists. Innocuous as it sounds, it drew huge criticism from the press and from economists – a mark, perhaps, of how far there was to go for the new philosophy to be understood, much less accepted.

It was not just economic policy that set Margaret Thatcher apart from many, if not most, in her party and led to division in the Shadow Cabinet. On immigration, she spoke about *colour-blind capitalism* in which she placed her faith. This was not the multi-culturalism of mainstream thinking: in this, as in issues of class or gender, Margaret Thatcher's credo was that people were worth something as individuals, and should be supported for their individual contribution, not because of their membership of a group. She was not in favour of Scottish devolution, which was a Heath pledge and a Callaghan/Wilson policy. She was 'ridiculously intransigent', as one senior Shadow Cabinet colleague despaired, against proportional representation when Lord Hailsham warned that the first-past-the-post system resulted in 'elective dictatorship'.[14] She was as adamantly opposed to a coalition government as she had been at the end of Heath's time in office.

It is tempting to see Margaret Thatcher during these years in the way in which she described herself in her memoirs, as a lone voice in the wilderness, single-mindedly preparing her party to follow her into government. Like many other things though, emergent Thatcherism was clearer in what it was against rather than what it was for, and less cohesive and coherent than it appeared. Some strands were clear, on both personal and political lines. Margaret Thatcher hated socialism, although she admired individual socialists like Clement Attlee. She reacted against collectivism emotionally

– to her, it was the antithesis of the solid middle-class values that she saw and prized in Grantham. She hated the politics of socialism, with its emphasis on collective workers' rights and government responsibility for intervention. She believed what she had read of Hayek and Solzhenitsyn who both saw the mechanisms of socialism as akin to those of slavery. She saw the work of Friedman and monetarist economics as the way forward, but was not yet able either to see or speak about how they might be implemented. Indeed, she may not have completely understood the concepts she was organising in her escape from socialism – certainly, her memoirs do not indicate the kind of theoretical understanding that would have made this possible. She was not an economist, she was a lawyer with the ability to master vast bodies of knowledge, but not necessarily great breadth of vision. Allied with economic fervour were a raft of beliefs and prejudices translated into policy. Absolute individualism can lead to individual policies: Margaret Roberts had seen widows forced to buy bruised fruit in her father's shop, and so, when cutting welfare, she protected widows' benefits. It did not occur to her that benefits as a whole should be protected, any more than it would have occurred to Alfred Roberts to give widows the bruised fruit from his shop for free. It was this difficulty in joined-up thinking, as much as the new ideas she was developing, that lead to uncertainty in her party.

But ready or not, united or not, the Conservative Party was soon to be embroiled in an election. They expected it to be called in October 1978, but at the last minute Callaghan changed his mind. This was a welcome reprieve for the Con-

'Labour isn't working.'

CONSERVATIVE SLOGAN, 1979

servatives – the summer of 1978 was perhaps the lowest period of the opposition years, with polls showing them lagging in popularity. Callaghan's stewardship was steady and conservative in a non-political sense. It was Margaret Thatcher, with her hatred of socialism, who seemed to be extreme. Her personal popularity rating was consistently lower than Callaghan's. The economic outlook was improving, and the April budget brought tax cuts.

But deferring the election turned out to be a bad move for the Labour Party. In January 1979, the lorry drivers went on strike, presaging the 'Winter of Discontent' with refuse collectors' strikes, miners' strikes, transport strikes, and even gravediggers' strikes. Margaret Thatcher's tough line on unions began to gain credibility in the party and in the country. In March, Margaret Thatcher forced a vote of no-confidence in the government. The announcement of a May election was inevitable. That March was perhaps the only time in her hard working and responsible life that Margaret Thatcher, preparing to give a television interview, became unavailable at the last moment. Two days after the announcement she was preparing for her first election address when she was told that a bomb had gone off under a car in the garage of the House of Commons. Airey Neave was dead. He was her friend and had supported her during her bid for leadership and the opposition years. Unlike the death of Ross McWhirter in 1975, whom she knew and liked and which had resulted in her being given police protection, this death was closer to home.

The 1979 election was Margaret Thatcher's one chance – and despite the loss of Airey Neave, she grasped it with both hands. This was the election where Saatchi and Saatchi used their famous advertising 'Labour isn't working' over pictures of an increasing queue at the labour exchange. She dominated the press campaign – making a point of reaching voters wherever possible. With Denis at her side, she rode the campaign bus and grabbed every photo opportunity available. But the key to this election was the new toughness in her manifesto about reform of trade union law. In the wake of the 'Winter of Discontent', and perhaps to the surprise of the Conservatives, Margaret Thatcher won the election and was Prime Minister.

Part Two

THE LEADERSHIP

Chapter 5: Thatcherism at Home

At 53 years of age, Margaret Thatcher was the first woman leader of a major Western democracy. She was proud of being the first chemist to do so. She represented a new political dawn – the first post-war prime minister to enter the job with a political philosophy that was actively opposed to collectivism. As Peregrine Worsthorne put it, she was the first political evangelist to occupy Downing Street since Labour's post-war landslide. She had spent 20 years in Parliament, but had held only one post in government.

The call from the Palace came at about 2.45 in the afternoon. There had already been celebration at Central Office, freesias everywhere, and a big chocolate cake shaped like the door of Number 10. Margaret Thatcher drove to the Palace with Denis. They returned in the Prime Ministerial car, and this time the guards saluted her. She was able to practise what she wanted to say as she walked through the crowds to Downing Street. Her opening speech is famous: *I know full well the responsibilities that await me as I enter the door of No. 10 and I'll strive unceasingly to try to fulfil the trust and confidence that the British people have placed in me and the things in which I believe. And I would just like to remember some words of St. Francis of Assisi which I think are really just particularly apt at the moment. 'Where there is discord, may we bring harmony. Where there is error, may we bring truth. Where there is doubt, may we bring faith. And where* there is despair, may we bring hope'... . And finally, one last thing: in the words of Airey Neave whom we had hoped to bring here with us, 'There is now work to be done'.[1] And work there was! Over the years, Margaret Thatcher had schooled herself to sleep for only four hours a night. Watching the election results she had only a couple of hour's rest.

The Downing Street staff met her at the door. There were familiar faces in the Cabinet Room including Carol Thatcher, back from Australia for the election. Alison Ward, her constituency secretary was there and so was Cynthia Crawford, her personal assistant. Margaret Thatcher's personal staff were concerned about which office to occupy: so was Mrs. Thatcher, with cabinet offices. The press expected a list of the new Cabinet within about 24 hours, and she needed to move fast. This was the first and last Chinese takeaway of her period in Number 10, eaten by about 15 of her closest advisers as they put together the new government.

'Where there is discord, may we bring harmony. Where there is error, may we bring truth. Where there is doubt, may we bring faith. And where there is despair, may we bring hope'

THATCHER

Some appointments were obvious. Geoffrey Howe was a true believer in monetarist economic policy, and was duly appointed Chancellor of the Exchequer. He became the longest serving member of her Cabinet. Keith Joseph, Margaret Thatcher's *closest political friend*,[2] went to Industry. Willie Whitelaw, who had pledged his loyalty to Mrs Thatcher, the party and the economic policy in 1974 and never withdrew it, Became Deputy Prime Minister. Margaret Thatcher called him *a big man, in character as well as physically*.[3] He was established with the Conservative 'old guard', and could have gathered enough of a following to cause real trouble. Instead, he became the lynch-pin of her first government.

Some people were necessary to retain party unity – Jim Prior was an important symbol, appointed to negotiate with the unions. *Yet there was no doubt in my mind that we needed Jim Prior ... Jim was the badge of our reasonableness.*[4] Although he had serious reservations about a monetarist cabinet, Peter Walker became Minister of Agriculture although he had made no secret of his opposition to her economic strategy. *His membership of the cabinet demonstrated that I was prepared to include every strand of Conservative opinion in the new government, and his post that I was not prepared to put the central economic strategy at risk.*[5] By 11 p.m. the list of Cabinet members was complete, and the Thatchers were driven home to Flood Street for some sleep. Margaret Thatcher was back early on Saturday to see the members and to oversee their 'swearing in'. Monday was a Bank Holiday. The first meeting was held on Tuesday afternoon. The Thatcher years had begun.

Mrs Thatcher also needed to move into Number 10. When she arrived, the area outside the Cabinet Room looked *rather like a down-at-heel Pall Mall club.*[6] This could be changed at once by using furniture from the rest of the house. More long-term alterations followed – original works of art instead of copies, her own collection of porcelain outside the flat, silver borrowed from Lord Brownlow to sparkle in the dining room. The private study was re-papered in cream, the better to show pictures. Flowers were displayed right up until the Thatchers left, 11 years later. Life 'above the shop' suited Margaret Thatcher. The flat at Number 10 is always described as 'poky', and is under the eaves in the rooms that would have been the servants' quarters in the original house. Denis and Margaret did not need domestic help. The deep freeze was always stocked, and there was always something to 'cut at' in the fridge, though it is unlikely either of the Thatchers organised such things. Margaret Thatcher did tidy up the clutter, and cook eggs and cheese, or 'Bovril toast'. Often, she would be fixing something to eat at 11 o'clock at night. She no longer needed the family breakfast: now, she would have toast, water and Vitamin C.

With the Cabinet in place, then came the programme. The overall majority of 43 allowed Margaret Thatcher to claim a mandate for her policies, and ensured that they would be passed by Parliament. The election result showed a division in the country. In the south, Conservatives had 186 seats compared to Labour's 30. In the north, Labour held 107 seats to the Conservatives' 53. The majority was sufficient, though, for Margaret Thatcher to begin the work that her convictions had led her to. Her economic policy took absolute priority through this first government.

The first duty of monetarists is to reduce the amount of money in the marketplace – literally to take currency out of use. If there is a lot of currency in use, then the principles of the marketplace imply that it will not have value. Therefore, the cause of inflation – the monster of the post-war years, where more actual money was constantly needed to pay for goods – was increases in the money supply. The government must stop spending money. They must remove subsidies to industry, reduce welfare spending, reduce government expenditure. The only money available to government was money taken from individuals through taxation: high taxation took away people's responsibility to spend their own money wisely. Some industries would go out of business, but they would be replaced by new, stronger, more profitable industries. In the meantime, there would be unemployment but it was not up to the government to prevent that. Nor was it up to the government to support people who could work if there were jobs.

Conflict with the trade unions was inevitable, but Margaret

Thatcher, bloodied by the fall of the Heath government, had no intention of taking them on except on her own terms. In her first Prime Minister's question time, asked about the unions, she said, *I am not confronting anyone*, and perhaps with more warning, *I hope that they are not confronting me, either.*[7] Jim Priors' employment bill, published at the end of the year, was cautious. First came the budget, in June. There were election pledges to be kept. Money had to be spent on defence, on public-sector wages, on old age pensions (although this was only a short-term expense: this budget broke the link between pensions and wages, making long-term savings possible). Spending on the National Health Service had to be protected for at least three years. Despite being boxed in by these considerations, Howe did manage to save considerable amounts from a variety of sources, including local government spending. Prescription charges were raised for the first time in eight years. The civil service was cut drastically, departmental budgets were cut, shares in public-sector assets were sold. These savings made room for tax cuts. Tax cuts were designed to shift responsibility for spending on health, welfare and entrepreneurial activity from the government to the individual – people with more money in their pockets would spend it on things they thought important. This benefited the economy. It also, as a matter of Thatcherite principle, benefited individuals by increasing their independence.

In the short term, these measures would increase inflation and unemployment. This was radical medicine, and signalled real change. The first casualty was the steel industry. Steel workers went on strike early in 1980. Thirteen weeks later, Keith Joseph made funds available to settle the dispute, but there were massive losses of customers at home and overseas. The government did not renew the subsidy to prevent the ensuing massive redundancies. The steel unions lost credibility in the face of huge unemployment. The monetarist point was made. Government was not going to provide full employment – only a competitive industry could survive. Competition meant that wages must remain within the parameters of possibility in a capitalist world: the government would not help employers pay more in wages than they earned in the marketplace.

Over the next two years the government's popularity fell as unemployment rose. There were riots in many inner-city areas – especially those with large immigrant populations, where unemployment was disproportionately high. Worse, there was no sign of inflation falling – in Thatcher's first year of office, it rose from 10.3 per cent to 21.0 per cent. The only possible remedy was to raise interest rates still further – against Margaret Thatcher's instincts, since it would also raise the cost of mortgages. Margaret Thatcher never wavered in public, but in private she was concerned. She knew that she needed at least two terms to put in place lasting reforms.

The lady's not for turning.

THATCHER

The 1980 Conservative party conference was painful, with rioters and protesters camped outside the doors and record levels of unemployment, bankruptcy and home repossessions. In her memoirs, Margaret Thatcher said: *Our strategy was the right one, but the price of putting it into effect was proving so high, and there was such limited understanding of what we were trying to do, that we had great electoral difficulties. However, I was utterly convinced of one thing: there was no chance of achieving that fundamental change of attitudes which was required to wrench Britain out of decline if people believed that we were prepared to alter course under pressure.*[8] She made the point in a line provided by Ronnie Millar: *The lady's not for turning.*

The critical period for economic policy came in 1981. The government's third budget was as stringently anti-Keynesian as the preceding ones, but there was rising concern in the party. If Willie Whitelaw, the Tory grandee, had joined the dissenters, it is extremely unlikely that Margaret Thatcher would have retained the leadership. But he didn't. In September she reshuffled her Cabinet. Lord Soames and Ian Gilmour were asked to resign. Mark Carlisle, who had fought for the education budget, made way for Keith Joseph. Nigel Lawson joined the Cabinet: Nicolas Ridley and Jock (now Lord) Bruce Gardyne joined the treasury, ensuring financial control by monetarists. This was also the moment to take a stand in employment. Jim Prior went to Northern Ireland. His team was broken up, and his place was taken by Norman Tebbit.

The way was now clear for the second strand of monetarism – strict limitation of the power of the unions. Freedom for employers to manage their workforce should be as complete as possible. The unions, with their ability to use industrial unrest as a way of demanding higher wages, were as big an interference in the free market as government subsidies had been. Conflict with the unions had brought down Heath's government while union action had caused the 'Winter of Discontent'. To Margaret Thatcher, the unions were as big a force for evil as socialism.

Electorally, the slide in Conservative fortunes began to slow in January 1982, despite unemployment standing at over three million. Perhaps sales of council houses helped. This was a very popular move, although Margaret Thatcher had initially had reservations about it. In 1975, she was arguing against substantial discounts because they were unfair to people who had bought unsupported in the private market – *What will they say on my Wates estates?*.[9] By 1979, the 'right to buy' was a manifesto commitment, introduced in the 1980 Housing Act. In October 1982, she was able to tell the party conference that *half a million people will now live and grow up as freeholders with a real stake in the country and with something to pass on to their children ... This is the largest transfer of assets from the state to the family in British History*.[10] Of course, a large part of what was being transferred were the houses built in Attlee's 'Jerusalem', so that every working person would have a home for himself and his family, paid for from taxation in a post-war economy. The best of these were sold quickly, to tenants with jobs. Rents on poorer housing increased as it became scarcer, and poorer or unemployed people were priced out of even the poorest estates. Council housing on any significant scale has not returned – profits from sales were ring-fenced, so that local authorities could not re-build.

If a general election had been called in early 1982, it is doubtful whether Margaret Thatcher would have been returned to power. Her radical alternative had been limited in this first term to a concerted attempt to limit the money supply by reducing subsidy to industry, transferring responsibility for welfare from the government to the individual by reducing taxation, and making some modest cuts in welfare spending. The immediate results were increasing hardship among poor people. She herself knew that she needed to have more than one term in office for the medicine to begin to work, and an electoral mandate to make the sweeping changes she believed were needed.

In April 1982, Argentina invaded the Falkland Islands, and Margaret Thatcher went to war. This was not part of an integrated foreign policy, but it was very much part of her personal credo. The lady who was not for turning and who had grown up believing that the British Empire was an absolute force for good and civilisation could not allow part of the British heritage to be lost through invasion. She was supported by Denis, who as an ex-military man reassured her that the war was winnable. It would be expensive, not only in monetary terms. For once, monetarism took a back seat in policy-making. Winning this war was both a personal and a national crusade. By mid-June the fighting was over and the war was won. The fallout from that victory continued throughout the remainder of Margaret Thatcher's career, not least in the form of Tam Dalyell's constant fight to prove that the initial act of war, the sinking of the Argentinean cruiser *General Belgrano* was unjustified. Her relationship with the BBC, whose even-handedness in calling forces 'Argentinian' instead of 'the enemy' she saw as being anti-war and anti-her, never recovered. The war was a Quixotic and romantic and very British escapade, full of sound and fury but gaining little or nothing. It did improve the image of British troops abroad – the conquest had been completed professionally and quickly. It did increase Margaret Thatcher's personal standing at home. It cost, when the immediate expense and the ongoing costs of supporting the Falklands and replacing ordinance lost is included, somewhere in the region of £3 billion, and 255 British servicemen were killed and 777 injured. When Margaret and Denis Thatcher visited the Islands, she saw a discarded ammunition case left to rust.

The *General Belgrano*, a former American heavy cruiser armed with 15 6-inch guns, was torpedoed and sunk by the British nuclear submarine HMS *Conqueror* at 16.00 hours on 2 May 1982: 321 lives were lost. As the ship and her escorts were outside the official exclusion zone established around the Falklands, this lead to the accusation that the sinking was unjustified. However, the cruiser was held to pose a threat to the British task force and the sinking drove the Argentinian surface fleet back into port for the rest of the war.

What a waste, she cried. 'For God's sake woman,' said Denis, 'don't get out and count them.'[11]

The war also took its toll on Margaret Thatcher. She was now 57 years old, and had been head of a government that was, at least for a while, one of the most unpopular ever. She was a very visible head, and worked as hard as she had done as an unknown backbencher. In the summer after the Falklands, she and Denis took a holiday in Switzerland. She then had an operation, privately, for varicose veins – a painful and debilitating procedure. During this time, the work on the manifesto for the next election continued. At the start of 1982, she was perhaps in danger of losing the possibility of a second term. This was unlikely now, and she must be ready to take advantage.

When Margaret Thatcher took the party to the polls in June 1983, their decisive majority of 144 was partly a response to a strong leader, who had not turned back from her economic policy and who had decisively won back British property and self-esteem in the South Atlantic. It was also partly because the right wing of the Labour Party had seceded and formed the Social Democratic Party in 1981, leaving the anti-Conservative vote split both in Parliament and in the country. On her part, she was starting to sense economic recovery. She now had a Cabinet made up in most important aspects of people who supported monetarism, although shortly after the election she replaced Geoffrey Howe as Chancellor with Nigel Lawson. Perhaps more importantly, the grocer's daughter from Grantham had seen her earliest beliefs in individual strength and heroism vindicated. The old rhymes from her childhood must have come back to her, stressing the need to take individual decisions and stand by them. Certainly in the second term she took on collectivism, socialism and the trade unions head-on. Her manifesto had three major strands

— control of the unions, privatisation, and control of local government. She dominated legislation, with her personal authority and stature.

The trade union battle soon began. In March 1984, the National Union of Mineworkers went on strike. Most coalmines were in the north of England, and Margaret Thatcher's Conservatives held few Northern seats. The miners, with their ability to control the fuel that was central to British industry, had proved themselves over and over again as the union force to be reckoned with. Margaret Thatcher knew that this was the union that would make or break monetarist policies. As early as 1981, she had begun quietly building up coal reserves in case of an industrial dispute. In 1983, she was ready. Ian McGregor, who had overseen the removal of subsidies from the steel companies, took over at the National Coal Board. His job was to decide what was to become of pits that were not profitable. Arthur Scargill, for the miners, argued that such pits could and should be made profitable with more investment: Ian McGregor, for the government, argued that a profitable industry relied on each and every pit being profitable. Unprofitable pits should be closed — otherwise, in Margaret Thatchers' words, mining would become a *system of outdoor relief*.[12] In March, the National Coal Board announced the closure of Cortonwood colliery in Yorkshire. It would have been in the Mineworkers' interests to delay any strike until the winter, but they were committed to the defence of all pits. They went on strike. The resulting battle was bitter and bloody — literally bloody. Police and miners fought at pit heads, and some miners and supporters lost their lives. The battle for public support was equally bloody. Margaret Thatcher's view that the BBC was left-wing and biased, formed during the Falklands War, was consolidated now. The strike lasted until March 1985, and ended in defeat for the miners. It opened the door for tougher legislation to control trade union action, already started by Jim Prior and continued by Norman Tebbit in 1982. Perhaps the most important limitations on the unions was the requirement to hold a secret ballot of members before any action, and limitations on the extent to which unions could work together. This, coupled with changes in the benefits system that removed benefits from strikers, allowed the government to control strikes and strikers.

The results of the policies were clear in the print strike. On 24 January 1986, some 6,000 trade unionists struck after months of protracted negotiation with their employers, News International and Times Group Newspapers. The company management was seeking a legally binding agreement at their new plant in Wapping which incorporated flexible working, a no-strike clause, new technology and the abandonment of the closed shop. Immediately after the strike was declared, the employers dismissed the striking workers and moved their major business to Wapping. There was a police presence to ensure that work continued, and in 1987 the strike collapsed. Two failed strikes and the government's policies, changed the face of trade unionism irrevocably.

Control of trade unions went side by side with the government programme of privatisation. This was a more far-reaching process than the simple removal of subsidies begun during the first term, but undertaken because of the same underlying philosophy. The government had no business being directly involved in the marketplace. Individuals should have the right to succeed, the incentive to work, and the ability to fail – otherwise they would never try. *Which is the better nurse?*, asked Margaret Thatcher in 1980, *the one who brings you all your meals, or the one who makes you shake out of it and put your feet to the floor?*[13] So the industries painstakingly nationalised since 1945, in order to ensure that all people had equal rights to benefits, were now returned to individual ownership. The railways, the Post Office, telephones, the electricity boards, gas, water – all would, in time, be returned to private ownership and so become open to competition. The public were given the opportunity to buy shares in the industries, and many did. For some, this was their first experience of owning shares and often a very lucrative one. Of course, others did not or could not buy shares. Nigel Lawson headed this programme of flotation on the stock market of previously nationalised industries, helped by a world wide favourable economic climate and fall in the price of oil. British Steel was used as an example: By 1989 the corporation that had lost one-third of its workforce was making as much steel as it had in 1979. Privatisation through share flotation was not a programme supported by all Conservatives – Lord Stockton, formerly Harold Macmillan, called it 'selling the family silver'. Margaret Thatcher replied *It is selling it back to the family.* She knew the policy was popular: *Share-ownership is up threefold since 1979. People who've bought shares in British Gas, British Telecom and the other highly successful privatised companies want to see how their shares are doing.*[14] There was at least a possibility that share ownership would give a bonanza to ordinary people.

Share-ownership is up threefold since 1979. People who've bought shares in British Gas, British Telecom and the other highly successful privatised companies want to see how their shares are doing.

THATCHER

The third strand of this manifesto was control of local authority power and spending. Again, this was a cause that was both personal and political. John Campbell talks about her hatred of local government as 'irrational, almost visceral dislike'.[15] He links it to the episode where her father was voted out of his position as alderman, and goes further – perhaps her dislike was a delayed revenge for what he saw as her repressed and joyless childhood. Certainly, she showed few signs of returning to Grantham after her marriage to Denis. However it is also true that during the bruising period before the 1983 election, Ken Livingstone's Labour Greater London Council was displaying the growing numbers of unemployed in floodlights on the roof of County Hall, across the river from Westminster. Six other Metropolitan Boroughs, also Labour-run, were ignoring spending restraints and education policy. The result was predictable. The seven city councils were abolished.

With manifesto commitments secured, it seemed an easy downhill run to the next election, at least on the home front. The 'blip' that arose on the horizon was called the Westland affair in the press, and resulted in open dissent in the Conservative Party. A small company manufacturing helicopters ran into financial difficulties. Michael Heseltine wanted to secure support from a European consortium in order to protect Britain's defence interests. The company looked towards American support. Margaret Thatcher argued that the government should not be involved in the choice, but privately favoured the American option. There were arguments, inside and outside Parliament. Michael Heseltine walked out of Cabinet, and two weeks later Leon Brittan also resigned. These two became formidable enemies to Margaret Thatcher in the future.

The election in June 1987 returned the Conservative government with a majority of 101. For the first few months after this election they were riding high in the opinion polls, and able to set about their manifesto commitments. This government intended to reform education, housing and health, all areas where collectivism seemed well entrenched. The economy was booming. Nigel Lawson, in his first budget, reduced the standard rate of income tax to 25 per cent – an all-time post-war low. More controversially, he reduced the top rate of tax from 60 per cent to 40 per cent – the rich no longer supported the poor.

The next few years were hard for Margaret Thatcher. She distrusted Lawson, whom she felt took too much credit for the economic gains of the party, and who would make a redoubtable opponent for the leadership. All was not well in the economy, either. In October 1987, 'Black Monday' saw the largest recorded fall in stock-market prices ever recorded. Lawson responded to the world-wide fall in shares by cutting interest rates. The long-term effect of this was to restore inflation, never absolutely defeated, by encouraging spending. In December, Willie Whitelaw suffered a slight stroke, and resigned in January 1988. However, in November 1988, all the key planks of the government's programme were unveiled. First, housing reform spelled the end of council housing: Housing Action Trusts (HATs) were introduced to improve run down estates by converting them to private ownership. Over the Thatcher years, the sale of good-quality council houses to working people had forced poor people to live in poorer housing: increases in rent had made more people dependent on housing benefit. Where there were still council housing estates, often in job-poor areas of Britain, they were occupied by poor families drawing housing benefit. These families saw no advantage in swapping the council they knew for the HAT they did not. The largest category of housing need at this time was the shocking increase in visible homelessness, not the poor in poor-quality housing. Welfare cuts had removed benefit entitlement from several categories, particularly young people and single unemployed people. The million council houses that had been sold had not been replaced in any way. Rents in remaining housing and the private rented sector had risen out of reach for such people. Margaret Thatcher was not unaware of the problem, but did not regard it as one a government should solve: *This year [1990], we are increasing from £600,000 to £2 million the support we give to voluntary organisations who help and advise the homeless. Much of this money will go to advisory services, so that fewer young people leave home without making proper arrangements about where to live.* In her memoirs, she made it clear that young people should be at home with their families, and that the government had no right to interfere with family life. It was this belief that fuelled changes in the welfare benefit scheme that reduced benefits for young and unemployed people, providing some relief for the disabled and the 'deserving' poor – people who had worked.

Second, there was reform of the National Health Service. Margaret Thatcher would have liked to move away from a tax-funded service but the electorate would not accept that. The tension resulted in the introduction of 'internal markets' in the Health Service – division between the providers of essential service and the purchasers of those services. Bevan had set up the health service so that all the essential goods needed to provide health care would be the property of the health service – they would own the beds, the towels, the services of the cleaners. He believed that this would make health care as cheap as possible. Now Margaret Thatcher introduced competition in provision of those services, so that the price could be driven down. Bevan had believed that lack of competition would ensure good cheap services: Margaret Thatcher believed exactly the opposite.

Reform of education was also a manifesto commitment, and a problem. Margaret Thatcher's time as Secretary of State for Education had not changed her fundamental view that education should be the transfer of a body of knowledge, and that schools that took a pupil-centred approach were contributing to the creation of a lazy and under-qualified population. Kenneth Baker was charged with steering the Great Education Reform Bill – known all too soon as the 'GERBIL', through Parliament. This was really five separate bills, each one of which was a substantial measure in itself. One set up a national curriculum for all schools to follow – which caused conflict between Margaret Thatcher, Baker and educationalists everywhere in deciding what was, and what was not, good education. Another gave schools the right to 'opt out' of local authority control. She hoped that most schools would take this choice, and that local authorities would lose power in education. In fact, in 1990 only about 50 schools in the country did so. Another bill established 'City Technology Colleges' as an alternative to comprehensive education, but only 15 were ever set up. In higher education, the difference between universities and polytechnics was abolished, facilitating a huge increase in student numbers – from 700,000 in 1988 to one million in 1993. Finally, the Inner London Education Authority was disbanded. This had survived the abolition of the Greater London Council to provide co-ordination for education services in schools across the capital, but it was expensive and, in Margaret Thatcher's eyes, unrepentantly Labour-run. Passing all of these reforms together took up 370 hours of parliamentary time – a post-war record.

By 1990, though, bigger problems were stalking Margaret Thatcher. In 1974, as Shadow Environment Secretary, she had first looked with distaste at the rating system in England and Wales. Now, she had the opportunity to do something about it. The Community Charge (or 'Poll Tax'), was introduced in April 1990 to replace domestic rates. In theory it simply shifted the levy required by local government from property to individuals. It charged a flat resident's charge per head for every adult – so the richest adult was charged the same amount as the poorest. Charging individually instead of by address caused huge injustices – some groups benefited while poorer households suffered. The Conservatives' own figure indicated that seven out of ten people would be worse off – but these were not people in large houses in wealthy areas. Riots and the biggest wave of civil disobedience ever seen in Britain followed. Lawson had argued against the Poll Tax, the only one of the Cabinet to do so.

In July 1990, the IRA struck again, killing Margaret Thatcher's friend and ally Ian Gow. He had been her first Parliamentary Private Secretary, and had argued for monetarist policies in the long-ago Heath years. He and Margaret Thatcher formed a close friendship, and he was renowned for pressing her interests in Parliament and the Parliamentary party. He was killed by a car bomb outside his home. Margaret Thatcher remembered: *I could not help thinking* ... *that my daughter Carol had travelled with Ian in his car the previous weekend to take his dog out for a walk: It might have been her too.*[16] That day she attended the Catholic Church where Gow and his wife were parishioners, and was moved by the response to his death.

M. Delors, said at a press conference the other day that he wanted the European Parliament to be the democratic body of the community, he wanted the commission to be the executive and he wanted the council of Ministers to be the Senate. No. No. No.

THATCHER

The final straw came not from domestic policy but from the European Union. In October 1989, Lawson resigned, citing differences with Margaret Thatcher about the European Exchange Rate Mechanism (ERM) – an early sign of storms ahead. In October 1990, the European Council held in Rome had pressed the case for a single currency. Government policy,

'The second thing that happened was, I fear, even more disturbing. Reporting to this House, my right hon. Friend almost casually remarked that she did not think that many people would want to use the hard ecu anyway – even as a common currency, let alone as a single one. It was remarkable – indeed, it was tragic – to hear my right hon. Friend dismissing, with such personalised incredulity, the very idea that the hard ecu proposal might find growing favour amoung the peoples of Europe, just as it was extraordinary to hear her assert that the whole idea of EMU might be open for consideration only by future generations. Those future generations are with us today. How on earth are the Chancellor and the Governor of the Bank of England, commending the hard ecu as they strive to, to be taken as serious participants in the debate against that kind of background noise? I believe that both the Chancellor and the Governor are cricketing enthusiasts, so I hope that there is no monopoly of cricketing metaphors. It is rather like sending your opening batsmen to the crease only for them to find, the moment the first balls are bowled, that their bats have been broken before the game by the team captain.

The point was perhaps more sharply put by a British business man, trading in Brussels and elsewhere, who wrote to me last week, stating: "People throughout Europe see our Prime Minister's finger-wagging and hear her passionate, 'No, No, No', much more clearly than the content of the carefully worded formal texts."

... The tragedy is – and it is for me personally, for my party, for our whole people and for my right hon. Friend herself, a very real tragedy – that the Prime Minister's perceived attitude towards Europe is running increasingly serious risks for the future of our nation. It risks minimising our influence and maximising our chances of being once again shut out. We have paid heavily in the past for late starts and squandered opportunities in Europe. We dare not let that happen again. If we detach ourselves completely, as a party or a nation, from the middle ground of Europe, the effects will be incalculable and very hard ever to correct.'

supported by Geoffrey Howe, was to suggest a parallel rather than a single currency, retaining national coins but using a 'hard ecu' as money across borders. Margaret Thatcher was prepared to support this, but she was still outspoken in her condemnation of the union. *The President of the Commission, M. Delors, said at a press conference the other day that he wanted the European Parliament to be the democratic body of the community, he wanted the commission to be the executive and he wanted the council of Ministers to be the Senate. No. No. No.*[17]

On 1 November 1990, Geoffrey Howe resigned. He used his resignation speech to criticise Margaret Thatcher, indict 'Thatcherism' and spell out the real differences between himself and Nigel Lawson, and the Prime Minister. It was, said Ronny Millar who had written Margaret Thatcher's speeches, 'A demolition job done with such meticulous artistry'.[18] This spelled the end. On 14 November, Michael Heseltine declared himself a candidate for the leadership of the party. Margaret Thatcher won the first ballot, but her lead was small. The Cabinet visited her one by one that night, advising her not to continue to a second ballot. Possibly for the first time in her life, Margaret Thatcher turned away from a direct challenge. On 22 November 1990, she resigned as Leader of the Conservative Party.

Chapter 6: Thatcher Abroad

In 1979, Margaret Thatcher's experience of foreign affairs was very limited. It was not her first priority – she would rather have got on with the job at home. Her upbringing in Grantham, the centre of the world to her, reading and loving Kipling's view of England while the war raged outside, had left her with absolute conviction that Britain was great, and that its contribution to the world was a force for civilisation and for good. This colonialist view does not sit well with multiculturalism, or with the European Union for that matter. It changed over time, but reluctantly. The challenges to her government were huge: the European Union, postcolonial problems like Rhodesia, the Falklands and Hong Kong, arms and trade agreements with the Soviet Union and America, and the Irish question. None of these had a simple answer, but answer them she must. She had even less faith in Foreign Office answers than she had in any other branch of the Civil Service. By the end of her period in office, she travelled without taking Foreign Office personnel, although in 1979 she did not have that confidence. The result was a foreign policy that developed different answers for different situations, but was unified by her personal manner. Critics may claim that she responded to and articulated the concerns of middle-class Britain. She certainly set a new direction in foreign policy, marked by her own individual style.

She had little time to reflect. Elected in May 1979, the European elections were in June. These were the first elections where Euro-MPs were elected directly to the European Parliament, rather than being delegated from national parliaments. Her view of the EU was well known, and repeated to young Conservatives in June: *Conservative principles do not change when we cross the Channel. There must be a golden thread of consistency running through our policies for Britain and our policies for the European Community. During our own election campaign, we argued for reduced public spending, lower taxation, more effective competition and a relentless war on bureaucracy. We shall pursue these same objectives in Europe.*[1] To her, her first task was to put the British contribution onto the European Union agenda. Britain imported more goods than other countries, and so paid more in tariffs. On the other hand, the European Union budget disproportionately supported agriculture, and Britain had less agriculture than other countries. We paid out more, and received less. This was an unacceptable situation, and Margaret Thatcher was determined to use her first European Summit in Strasbourg to change it. She went armed with her usual encyclopedic knowledge of the problem and determination to be heard. She delayed dinner on the second day to raise it – *Argument always gives one an appetite*, she said.[2] This first meeting 'set the scene' for her dealings with Europe. She saw herself as a strong voice for Britain, other leaders saw her as strident and demanding. Disputes were going to continue – she did not agree with any moves for the European Parliament to take over functions of the British Parliament, or for the sovereignty of nation states to be subsumed by the EU. Other leaders saw Europe as much

Conservative principles do not change when we cross the Channel. There must be a golden thread of consistency running through our policies for Britain and our policies for the European Community

THATCHER

more than just a trading community, and France and Germany were already powerful allies.

At the next summit in Dublin, her single-mindedness meant that no work could be carried out unless and until the British claim for a rebate was discussed and agreed. She did not succeed this time, and the row over contributions rumbled on. In her view, the EU owed Britain a reduction of £1,000 million of 'our money'. This argument crystallized the personal and political position of Britain over this first term of office. Although the French president, Valéry Giscard D'Estaing, was a conservative he was *an Olympian, not a patrician* in Margaret Thatcher's eyes.[3] She meant that he used the prestige of his name and family history to exclude the grocer's daughter from informal gatherings, and pomp and circumstance to marginalise her at formal ones. She had much more in common politically with the socialist German Chancellor Helmut Schmidt. Only different views of Europe separated them: His vision was of a united and federal Europe, hers of a European Union supporting free trade and made up of independent nations. The two men were friends, and hugely influential in Europe. Margaret Thatcher was not a friend to either, and was fighting for influence in European decision-making. To the concern of the Foreign Office which would have liked a wider discussion and a less obdurate and focused approach, she made it clear that the question of Britain's economic contribution would be the single major issue in dealing with the European Union. Even the Cabinet wished to smooth over the issue. In May, she was forced to accept an interim agreement because the Foreign Secretary, Peter Carrington, told her he personally would accept no other course of action, and it was clear that at least six colleagues and 70 Tory MPs would support him. The issue of British rebate continues to rumble in the background of EU negotiations.

Before Dublin, and scarcely back from Strasbourg, she travelled to the economic conference in Tokyo for the group of seven principal western industrial powers (the G7). She attracted huge interest at this summit – as much or more for being a woman in a male enclave as for the role she took. For her part, she became irritated with the process, refusing to enter into the first-name jocularity of the world leaders and disinterested in the main business of oil pricing and control. On the way, she had an unscheduled dinner at Moscow airport with the Soviet Prime Minister Alexei Kosygin. Here there were two issues – current American policy was to agree arms limitation with the Russians and Margaret Thatcher disagreed with that (six months later, when Russia invaded Afghanistan, she felt vindicated). Secondly, there was the problem of Vietnamese refugees. Could Russia put pressure on its fellow communists in Vietnam? The short-term answer was no. Her third summit that year was to be held in Lusaka for the meeting of the Commonwealth heads of government.

Despite these high-profile pressures, the biggest issue of this first term was to find some resolution to the problem of Rhodesia. In 1965, the Rhodesian Prime Minister Ian Smith had made a unilateral declaration of independence from British rule, flouting the policy that former colonies would only be recognised as independent states if they had introduced democratic elections and majority rule. His minority white government had struggled on until 1979, when elections were held and Bishop Muzorewa was elected as head of a black government. To bring peace to the country, this government needed international recognition. Margaret Thatcher's first instinct was to support the bishop even though he had been elected while Robert Mugabe was still leading a terrorist force, and the rebels had not been in included in the process. The Foreign Office was convinced, and convinced her, that this government would never achieve recognition from the surrounding Black African states. To do nothing was impossible – the sanctions that had creaked on since 1965 were unpopular, and would probably not be renewed by her government. Her response was pro-active and brave. Conservative ministers talked to every important player – in contrast to her attitude in Ireland, this included Mugabe and other leaders of guerrilla forces. These discussions and Foreign-Office briefings changed her view of independence: before this point she had argued against extensions of freedom for Commonwealth countries. By 1985 her opinion had almost reversed, from the need to maintain Britain's colonies to – *in practice, if you are a parliamentary democracy, then the holding of them* [colonial territories] *really can only be a temporary thing, until you bring them to … those same institutions which protect their liberty, in the same way as we developed ours. So if you look at it philosophically, it could only be a temporary thing, not a power structure; and that, I think, was shown years ago as people went first from colonies to dominion status in the pre-war period.*[4]

In Rhodesia, willingness to grasp the nettle, change tack and take risks paid off: Britain took direct control of the country through the governorship of Christopher Soames while more elections were held. Soames and his wife moved to Rhodesia before any cease-fire had been declared, at some personal risk. On 18 April 1980, Rhodesia, governed by a democratically-elected Mugabe, received independence. The experience tested the relationship between her and Peter Carrington, the Foreign Secretary on whom much policy in this first term would rely. In her memoirs she describes a *heated exchange* on the long journey out, when he suggested that the best they could do was damage-limitation. At that time, she says, she had never heard that phrase, and she intended to do very much better than that.[5] While she continued to move away from the

Foreign Office, some individuals, including Carrington, could influence her. Rhodesia was a strange first task for a woman whose personal beliefs would argue for retaining Commonwealth countries under British rule, but a necessary resolution to the problem for which she received due credit.

By the time she embarked on her second term of office in June 1983, Margaret Thatcher was an experienced, if not popular, diplomat. She had scored success over Rhodesia, established a European refund to Britain, and of course had won absolute victory in the Falklands. After that war her confidence in the superiority of Britain was manifest: *I believe Britain has now found a role. It is in upholding International Law and teaching the nations of the world how to live.*[6] The lessons would not have included the inner-city riots and public opposition that marked the end of her first term in office. Her attitude to the peace was typically intransigent. As far as she was concerned, she was the victor, and the question was now settled. Argentina did not see it the same way. Arguments over supporting and owning the small Falkland Islands continued throughout her period in government and are not settled today.

From the first I regarded it as my duty to do everything I could to reinforce and further President Reagan's bold strategy to win the Cold War.

THATCHER

The victory was helped along by Ronald Reagan, US President since 1980 and a natural ally. With him, Margaret Thatcher formed the close friendship she lacked in Europe. This was a personal and political friendship: she liked Reagan, though she did not always trust him, and she was adamant that Britain and America were natural allies and that Britain owed America for its intervention into the world wars. More important, the Cold War between Britain and Russia was affecting British economy – current defence policy was to invest in nuclear weapons for Britain, but also to support America, while America contributed to Britain's defence. Deterrence depended on a strong America. Her memoirs say: *From the first I regarded it as my duty to do everything I could to reinforce and further President Reagan's bold strategy to win the Cold War.*[7]And she did not move from that position, even when the Americans invaded Grenada, a British protectorate, without telling her. Worse, they told the Foreign Office they were not going to invade, leaving the Foreign Secretary to give misleading information to the House. This was tricky for Margaret Thatcher. She was furious with Washington: Hugo Young describes her as 'incandescent'.[8] Not only had Reagan humiliated her, America had also broken international law. Washington had thought that she would support the invasion, aimed as it was at unseating a Marxist government. But as far as she was concerned – *I think as a general rule we in the Western countries, the Western democracies, use our force to defend our way of life, we do not use it to walk into other people's countries, independent sovereign territories. We try to extend our beliefs not by force but by persuasion. So there is a general rule that you do not cross into an independent sovereign country. It's not an inviolate rule, but it's a very, very good one. I think, therefore, that if you're going to go into an independent sovereign country – and don't forget Grenada was given independence in 1974 with a fully independent constitution with a legal system, with democracy, it had gone by 1979 when Maurice Bishop seized power as a Marxist – but I think it's a good fault not to walk into another person's country and therefore, let me put it this way … you have to be absolutely certain that if you do there is no choice, or if there is no other way… . You mentioned oppression, Communism – yes, I hate it. There are many, many peoples in countries in the world who would love to be free of it, love to be free of it, that doesn't mean to say that we can just walk into them and say now you are free, I'm afraid.*[9] This was an answer

Ronald Reagan and George Bush

There is probably no more special a relationship in the 20th-century history of the Special Relationship between Britain and the United States than that between Mrs Thatcher and Ronald Reagan. *I had been immediately struck by his warmth, charm and complete lack of affectation*, she wrote in her memoirs. *Above all, I knew that I was talking to someone who instinctively felt and thought as I did; not just about policies but about a philosophy of government, a view of human nature, all the high ideals and values which lie – or ought to lie – beneath any politician's ambition to lead his country.*

It may be that one reason why President Reagan and I made such a good team was that, although we shared the same analysis of the way the world worked, we were very different people. He had an accurate grasp of the strategic picture but left the tactical detail to others. What Thatcher is implying is that Reagan left it to her, especially when it came to the handling of the Soviet Union or Europe. *I was conscious that we must manage our relations with the communists on a day-to-day basis in such a way that events never got out of control.* (The Downing Street Years, p 324.) Did Reagan ever resent being lectured to by the junior partner in the Special Relationship? He signed a photograph of the two of them at dinner at Number 10 in July 1988: 'Dear Margaret – As you can see, I agree with every word you are saying. I always do. Warmest Friendship. Sincerely Ron.'

After the Iraqi invasion of Kuwait a different picture emerges: *For all the friendship and co-operation I had had from President Reagan, I was never taken into the Americans' confidence more than I was during the two hours or so I spent that afternoon at the White House ... The President that day was an altogether more confident George Bush than the man with whom I had had earlier dealings. He was firm, cool, showing the decisive qualities which the Commander-in-Chief of the greatest world power must possess. Any hesitation fell away. I had always liked George Bush. Now my respect for him soared.* (The Downing Street Years, p 820.)

which also showed her usual detailed briefing. Her friendship with President Reagan did not seriously falter, however.

In the same week, there were massive demonstrations in London against the arrival of US cruise missiles in Britain. The Grenadian action could have threatened that decision, not least because it strengthened American opinion. She knew this, but did not hesitate: *We have a job to do here. We have to get Cruise missiles sited in pursuit of the NATO decision. We have to take the lead in doing it… . It was the most important thing in East/West terms and that you do not in fact put in jeopardy. All right, things somehow changed on the Monday* [invasion of Grenada], *they did not tell us anything over the weekend. But even then you just go back and look at the very first principles.*[10]

Later, and again against the advice of her Cabinet and public opinion, she supported the American bombing of Libya. In a response to Neil Kinnock at question time she said: *I remind him again that the United States, our staunch ally, keeps over 330,000 troops in Europe to defend the freedom of Europe and that, without the United States and Britain, Europe would not today be free. We must continue to keep that Alliance.*[11] This summed up her personal and political view that America deserved and should have absolute British loyalty, and that Britain would benefit from this special relationship. In 1991, she committed British forces without hesitation to the first Gulf War, to fight with the Americans and the other Coalition forces.

The relationship with Reagan was fundamental to the relationship with Soviet Russia, and here great things were happening. In 1983, Francis Pym went to the Soviet Union in a first small attempt to break the frozen impasse of the 'Cold War'. Margaret Thatcher was becoming convinced that it was necessary to talk to the Soviet Bloc, and so was Ronald Reagan. This was a huge change for both leaders. Reagan had been used to calling the Soviet bloc the 'focus of evil' in the modern world, and Margaret Thatcher had horrified her diplomats with her outbursts ever since the 'Iron Lady' speech in the 1970s. Now though, she was convinced that the advantages of the free market would be evident, if Communist leaders had the opportunity to experience them. Perhaps innocently, but very patronisingly, she made this absolutely clear: *they do not know how to think in any other terms and that, really, is one of the reasons why I invited Mr. Gorbachev here long before he is where he is now, because I wanted to be able to get some of the younger people up to show them how very much better a free society works. They may not understand how it works, but they can see how it works. They can see the massively increased prosperity.* [12]

Her relationship with Gorbachev was crucial to defusing the Cold War. She met him shortly after she visited Hungary, at the funeral of the Soviet president Yuri Andropov. Her view, that Communism could not contain its people for ever, was explicit. In October 1982, she visited the Berlin Wall and said: *Every decade since the war the Soviet leaders have been reminded that their pitiless ideology only survives because it is maintained by force. But the day comes when the anger and frustration of the people is so great that force cannot contain it. Then the edifice cracks: the mortar crumbles ... One day liberty will dawn on the other side of the wall.* [13]

One day liberty will dawn on the other side of the wall.

THATCHER

But the cost of defence spending to continue the Cold War was prohibitive, and something had to be done. This was agreed on both sides of the Atlantic – Reagan was writing to his Soviet opposite numbers at this time, but getting no response. In December 1984, she invited Gorbachev and his wife to Chequers. She had a wide-ranging discussion with him – Denis was also charming to and charmed by Gorbachev's wife, Raisa. The scene was set for discussion when Gorbachev later became Soviet leader in 1985.

Her preparations were almost torpedoed by America's 'Star Wars' initiative – a research programme intended to develop a new space-based anti-missile system that would make ballistic missiles obsolete. This possibility worried Europe, who saw themselves caught between two warring powers. It undermined nuclear deterrence, in which Margaret Thatcher believed and in which she had invested considerable money. Worse, it was clear that the Soviets would retaliate by creating equal weapons. Reagan and Gorbachev were meeting, and their discussion included phasing out nuclear weapons. This was wholly against Margaret Thatcher's beliefs – she truly believed that peace lay in the 'stand off' of equal nuclear armament, and she had invested a great deal of British money in Trident ballistic missiles. If she was to prevent the Soviet Union from withdrawing from arms talks and America retreating into isolationism she had little time. On the Sunday, she saw Gorbachev at Chequers. On Wednesday, she was in Beijing signing the agreement by which Hong Kong was returned to the Chinese. On Thursday, she was in Hong Kong reassuring the population. On Saturday, she was at Camp David to meet with President Reagan. In 1984 the journey was mammoth, the travelling uncomfortable, and each meeting vital. Her visit to America cemented the relationship with the USA, re-assured Europe, and elicited public statements that reassured the Russians. This was only one step on the path to discussion between America and Russia: The importance of nuclear deterrence was *the one issue on which I knew I could not take the Reagan Administration for granted*.[14]

By 1990, and before her resignation, the Berlin Wall had come down and Germany was reunified. There is no doubt that Margaret Thatcher's personal style was central to this process.

She was well aware of the danger of opening dialogue with the East and mediating their position with America: if America and the Soviet Union made a private deal, Britain and Europe could well be marginalised. If Russia and America agreed between them to abandon nuclear weapons, then Britain's arsenal would be an expensive white elephant, and Britain would be defenceless to other forms of attack. She knew that her personal friendship with Reagan would not, on its own, prevent this from happening: it was in American interests to find a way of ending the existing nuclear stalemate. Faced with a problem, Margaret Thatcher used her own well-honed skills to solve it – she went out to canvas. Starting in Hungary, she and her ministers set out to encourage Eastern bloc people to see the British Prime Minister as the embodiment of the benefits of capitalism. In Moscow, she went on a 'walkabout' in a Moscow housing estate – 'it almost appeared that the Prime Minister was fighting a by-election in Moscow North' one commentator remarked. 'Margaret Thatcher,' said another, 'in her Aquascutum wardrobe careering around the outer tenement blocks was one of the most impressive examples of political canvassing ever seen.'[15] The results were beyond even her imaginings – *I do not see ... that there will be anything other than a Communist system in the Soviet Union in my lifetime*,[16] she said in this year. Acting as friend to both Russia and America meant that British interests could be defended: failing to do so could mean that Britain was pinned between the two. But this also took her and Britain on a different path from the other European states.

During her second term, relations with Europe improved slightly, if only temporarily. Margaret Thatcher wanted Europe to be a trading community, with few trade barriers and little intervention in the market. The idea of a single market-place, where different nations could buy and sell without hindrance, was her free-market dream. Pressing ahead with the single market was the common factor between the leaders: in 1986, the 'Single European Act' was signed. But France and Germany had a different understanding of a single market – they foresaw, and looked forward to, harmonization of social policies as well as trade. The European heads of state distrusted Margaret Thatcher's friendship with America – she still regarded Europe as needing to be grateful for Britain and America's help in the war. *After all we* [Britain and America] *saved all their skins collectively in the war.*[17] she was reported as saying privately. Personally, her position was eased by the election of François Mitterrand as President of France. Although he was a socialist, they got on unexpectedly well. But she never considered Europe to be more than a free-trade area, and her opposition to closer European union was a strong as ever.

The necessary second step after a single market was agreed was de-regulation of prices and industrial relations. The step after that was integration of policy and practice, on ground that had been the prerogative of national governments. Some of this she should have known – for instance in 1987 it was agreed to harmonise VAT rates. Margaret Thatcher had to be forcibly reminded that provision for this was in the Treaty of Rome, and that she had been in the Cabinet that signed the treaty. The other leaders had no doubts: To them, the Single European Act signaled harmonization and integration across Europe. This came to a head in 1991, when other European heads of state signed the 'Social Chapter' of the Maastricht Treaty including a direct intention to implement the Community Charter of Fundamental Social Rights and requiring that social policies should be integrated across Europe. To Margaret Thatcher, this was a return to the support for workers' rights that she had defeated at home:

if legislation protected working hours, minimum standards, and health and safety practices then the employer, the industrialist, could not manage his own business. British opposition meant that an opt-out clause was included, although only Britain refused to sign.

A third problem left over from the colonial days, like Rhodesia and the Falklands, was Hong Kong. For 150 years the city had been a British protectorate, and an island of capitalism in a sea of communism. The lease on Hong Kong was due to expire in 1997. In 1983, she was reassuring the British public that talks were under way, and that the Hong Kong way of life would continue. *It will be quite tragic if between us, between China and Britain, we cannot make an arrangement which enables that way of life, that stability and prosperity, to continue, because it's compounded of two things – the enormous enterprise, hard work, inventiveness of the Chinese character in Hong Kong, and the system which has been run under the British in Hong Kong. Now it's trying to get the continuity of that system, together with the wonderful character of the Chinese people that we're struggling to maintain.*[18]

After 1984, she embarked on a series of speeches designed to reassure Hong Kong residents and the world. In Hong Kong itself she stressed three principles: *The first point I wish to make about this Agreement is that it assures the continuation of Hong Kong as a free trading capitalist society for a very long time to come – into the middle of the next century. This means that Hong Kong can plan long-term with confidence. I believe Chairman Deng* [Deng Xiaoping] *intends his bold concept of 'one country-two systems' to last. My second point is that you have my absolute assurance that Britain will administer Hong Kong wisely and well between now and 1997. We shall honour our obligations to the full. My third point is that Britain will not merely do all in its power to work for Hong Kong's steady development and a smooth transition; we shall also seek to win the widest possible acceptance of the Agreement in the rest of the world.*[19] The agreement was broadly accepted, and was carried out. These negotiations were different from both her obduracy in the Falklands, and her boldness in Rhodesia. Her major concern was that capitalism should continue: once she felt that aim had been met, her primary interest ended.

A constant thread throughout her office, and indeed her political life, was the vexed question of Northern Ireland. The Irish Republican Army touched her life very directly, in the death of Ross McWhirter, which resulted in her being given a police guard that is still with her: in the death of Airey Neave, her close friend and ally;[20] in the bombing of the Brighton hotel where she and her Cabinet were staying in 1984, injuring Norman Tebbit and his wife and killing five; at the end of her government, when Ian Gow was killed at his home. There were other high profile actions less close to her – the year that she entered office as Prime Minister was also the year that Lord Mountbatten and 18 soldiers were killed on the same day.

True to her background, Margaret Thatcher was staunchly Unionist – it would be surprising if she had not supported a largely Protestant movement that wished to retain close ties with Britain and British history. This would be the same argument as that which took her to the Falklands to protect the people, and made her prioritize Hong Kong people and their rights to capitalism. In opposition, in the unsanctioned speech that made her the 'Iron Lady' she made her views clear. *But we cannot afford, in Labour's view, to maintain our defences at the necessary level – not even at a time when on top of our NATO commitments, we are fighting a major internal war against terrorism in Northern Ireland, and need more troops in order to win it.*[21] To call the situation 'war' was a major slip: in government policy, it was always referred to as troops supporting the civilian government. But it made her position clear, and presaged the 21st-century 'War on Terror' fought today.

Unsurprisingly, Margaret Thatcher's public statements promised that Ireland would remain British for as long as the majority of her people wished it to. This was one area where she did not benefit from her usual meticulous briefings. The BBC's political editor John Cole, a Protestant Ulster man who could be expected to be sympathetic to her view, wrote that she had 'a total lack of feeling for a province that was remote from her own background'.[22]

More revealing, off-the-cuff remarks, that Irish Prime Minister Garrett Fitzgerald reports her making in 1985 when the Anglo-Irish Agreement was signed and Ireland was eligible for European Union funds, show her as disliking Irish demands: *More money for those people? Why should they have more money? I need that money for my people in England.*[23] Her choice of Northern Ireland secretaries did not dispel the picture. Airey Neave, in opposition, was a right-wing Unionist with only a nod towards nationalist views: his successors were little different. Margaret Thatcher took the killing of Lord Mountbatten with her customary courage and defiance. She flew to Ireland, did a walkabout in Belfast, and was photographed in a combat jacket and Ulster Defence Force beret. She went again at Christmas, and visited almost every year of her term of office.

In 1980, Charles Haughey took over as Irish Taoiseach. Margaret Thatcher liked him, staunch Nationalist though he was. The reports of their first meeting were positive: 'British sources agreed that a good personal relationship had been struck between the two prime ministers. They were now to hold regular meetings for the first time. But Mr. Haughey, while meticulously observing the confidentiality of the meeting, trumped all that by his bold performance. He said it was the most successful meeting he had had with any politician before an international news conference.'[24] When talks in December were reported equally positively, Margaret Thatcher wrote reassuringly to the Unionist leader the Reverend Ian Paisley: *Finally, let me stress that it remains a fundamental assumption of all government thinking on these matters that Northern Ireland is part of the United Kingdom and will remain so unless its people and the Westminster Parliament decide otherwise. I could hardly have made that clearer than I have done in recent days both in the House of Commons and outside it.*[25]

All this in the shadow of the hunger strikes by Republican prisoners seeking for recognition that they were prisoners of war. Asked on television whether she was willing to see an 'endless procession of young Irish men die', she replied: *That is a matter for those who go on hunger strike and those who are encouraging them to do so. I am not urging them to go on hunger strike. I am urging them not to die. I am urging them to choose the way of life and not the way of death. What I am saying and I believe I have the whole population behind me, I am saying I will not give political status or special category status to people who are in fact criminals and who are the enemies of society.*[26] Her ruthlessness was breathtaking. 1981 was the year that mainland Britain saw riots in Brixton and Toxteth, her personal popularity was at an all-time low, there were 73 deaths in Ireland, and seven hunger strikers died. The strike was finally called off in October. Was this a victory? It impressed the American government, but American money continued to flow to the IRA. It ensured her reputation for determination but Bobby Sands, the first striker to die, became a martyr to the Republican cause. Public opinion

It remains a fundamental assumption of all government thinking on these matters that Northern Ireland is part of the United Kingdom and will remain so unless its people and the Westminster Parliament decide otherwise.

THATCHER

had seen young Irish men die, and blamed her. Furthermore Haughey supported General Galtieri during the Falklands War.

In her second term, Fitzgerald returned as Taoiseach. Disappointed in Haughey, Margaret Thatcher got on better with him. In 1983 she authorised the preparation of secret proposals to end the impasse. On 17 December of that year, the IRA left a bomb outside Harrods department store in London, killing three shoppers and two policemen. But Margaret Thatcher was becoming more aware of the nuances of the Irish situation, and beginning to believe with her customary passion that the law-abiding constituency of nationalistic Catholics should be represented and reconciled with the British state. Northern Ireland was also straining her special relationship with Ronald Reagan – with Irish Catholic in his own background, he was susceptible to the American lobby that saw Britain as a colonial power in Ireland. Also, much as she disliked the Foreign Office, she was swayed by their argument that no solution could be found without the support of all of the Northern Irish population.

This could all have been derailed by the bomb at the Grand Hotel in Brighton on 12 October 1984 during the Conservative Party conference. She was extremely lucky to escape that attack without serious injury. Millar, who had just left her after a session on her speech, describes her sitting very still in the secretaries' room – *I think that was an assassination attempt, don't you?*[27] she said finally. Her first thought had been for Denis, who was asleep in the bedroom and unhurt. In her memoirs, she talks about the importance of the lights remaining on. For some months afterwards she slept with a torch by her bed.[28] She refused to be taken to Number 10 for safety that night. She had a copy of her speech, rescued by Millar and the secretaries – she was determined to give it. Her personal assistant, Cynthia Crawford, had collected some clothes – Margaret Thatcher was still in the ball gown she had been wearing earlier. Denis had dressed and collected a spare pair of shoes, worn later by the American Ambassador who had lost his. She slept that night in a twin room at the police training college in Lewes, with Crawford. Denis shared a room with the detectives. She woke up to the six o'clock news, and saw images of Norman Tebbit and his wife injured and trapped in the rubble. She was interviewed by the BBC and at 9.30 exactly she was walking onto the conference platform. Many of the people with her had lost their clothes, but Marks and Spencer's had opened early and it was an impressive turnout that opened that day of the conference.

She had spent the night adapting the speech – *We removed most of the partisan sections of the speech: this was not a time for Labour-bashing but for unity in defence of democracy.*[29] On the other hand there were tough sections on law and order that could stay. *I knew*, she said in her memoirs, *that far more important than what I said was the fact that I, as Prime Minister, was there to say it.*[30] She was there to say it, looking immaculate and never faltering. It was a performance worthy of the Britain she knew and admired, the Britain that had survived worse bombing than this during the Blitz. After the conference she went to the hospital to visit the injured. From there she spent 'hours' on the phone to find doctors with the expertise they needed – in the end, she found a doctor from El Salvador with earthquake experience. Then it was back to Chequers – faster than she had ever been driven in her life and with a full motorcycle escort. Emma Nicolson, an admirer of the early Thatcher, felt she was never the same again after the bomb. She became locked away from people, unable to see and hear and touch her admirers.

In the short term, relations with Ireland were difficult. A unified Ireland was out. Confederation of the two states was out. Joint authority was out. There would be no derogation from sovereignty. But, in November 1985, the Anglo-Irish Agreement was signed. The deal gave the Irish Republic a consultative role in Northern Ireland, setting up an inter-governmental conference of ministers and civil servants with its own secretariat. No future changes would be made without a democratic vote. It was a bargaining position to maintain security, not the end result either side wanted. It failed to deliver cross-border cooperation on security, and the 'war' with the IRA continued. In 1987, she prevailed on Douglas Hurd to ban the broadcasting of the voices of Sinn Fein or the IRA. This was a double-edged sword – broadcasters used actors to speak the words, and by so doing increased the cred-ibility of the comments. By 1993, she was convinced that the Agreement had been a fundamental mistake. She argued for an alternative, but neither had an alternative nor had the time in office to find one. Successive governments had not found a better approach, and despite her intentions rather than because of them the Agreement has been the foundation of a slow process leading to peace.

When she left government, Margaret Thatcher had reached a conclusion to many of the big issues of her day. The Falklands rumbled on, and future events in Rhodesia dis-credited the Mugabe government, but neither of these were a direct result of her intervention. Only her issues with the European Union have proved insuperable. Her views were well known. She had spoken in favour of a union for free trade, and been blind to the potential of any other union, from the earliest days of Heath's government. She bent in other areas – for instance in the need to consult Nationalists in Northern Ireland, or not to recognise Bishop Muzorewa's government in Rhodesia, but she never changed her view of Europe. The big questions of Europe – how far Britain should be part of the European Union, or indeed what the purpose of the European Union was – are still not agreed by the Conservative Party. Margaret Thatcher was obdurate, but for some parts of her period of office sufficient members of the party agreed with her to make her position tenable if not secure. In the end, the final argument with Howe over the single currency was the catalyst that ended her government. Perhaps if it had not been Europe it would have been some other thing, and certainly she was unpopular in the country and with the party. It almost seems unfair that the policy that unseated her was one of the clearest and most straightforward parts of her personal manifesto.

Part Three

THE LEGACY

Chapter 7: After Thatcher

Leaving office was hard for Margaret Thatcher. She would never again be the centre of power and attention. There is no obvious role for an ex-prime minister, now 66 years old but with no intention of retiring. It might have been easier if she had been overthrown in an election – then she would have been prepared to move out of Downing Street. As it was, her daily routine and importance vanished overnight. She saw the Cabinet's advice to stand down as treachery. Her exit from Downing Street was tearful. Cynthia Crawford began packing immediately, but the flat had to be emptied quickly. She had one last weekend at Chequers to collect all the personal belongings of 11 years of Thatcher residency. Her last duty, as she describes it in her memoirs, was to ensure that John Major rather than Heseltine succeeded her.[1] He was duly elected leader after the second ballot, and she left Number 10 on Wednesday 28 November with a typical farewell speech for the cameras – *Now is the time for a new chapter to open and I wish John Major all the luck in the world*[2] – and set off to start a new life in Dulwich, in the house she and Denis had bought overlooking the Dulwich and Sydenham golf course.

Public honours followed. In December 1990, she was granted the Freedom of Westminster, an honour previously only given to Winston Churchill. The Queen awarded her the Order of Merit – the highest honour that is in the royal gift.

There can be only 24 members of the order at any one time – Laurence Olivier had died, leaving a vacancy for Margaret Thatcher. In 1992, she was created Baroness Thatcher, of Kesteven in the County of Lincolnshire, and entered the House of Lords. In addition, Denis Thatcher was given a Baronetcy (ensuring that their son, Mark, would inherit a title). But honours do not substitute for a job, and there simply was no job for her. With some prescience, in 1987, she said of cabinet ministers who were shuffled out of office: *But also there is one other thing which has bothered me such a great deal. It is the only job, I think in the United Kingdom, under which you do not get any severance pay or notice at all. I must say I find this inhuman.*[3] At first she had no staff, and could not even answer the thousands of letters arriving to offer her sympathy. She was essentially an unemployed workaholic. She was very unlikely to take herself out of the public eye – even if the public, who had loved her and hated her with passion over the course of her career but had never been indifferent, would have let her.

She was not retiring to a family home or to close relationships with her children. She adored Mark and would not hear a word against him, but the relationship had cooled over the last few years. He left Harrow in 1971 with just three O-levels, did not go to university and failed his accountancy exams three times. He went through a series of short-term jobs, and has been the subject of allegations and litigation over questionable business dealings. In 1994, he went to live in South Africa and has rarely returned to England. He has been linked to controversial dealings abroad, and was arrested on suspicion of involvement in planning a coup in Africa. That year, Margaret

It is the only job, I think in the United Kingdom, under which you do not get any severance pay or notice at all. I must say I find this inhuman.

THATCHER

Thatcher defended him publicly, and visited him and met her 18-month-old granddaughter for the first time while collecting an honorary degree in Houston. She has seen little more of Carol Thatcher, who has recently appeared on reality television shows, and has been quoted as saying that Mark was always the favourite.[4] She got excellent A-levels, studied Law, and then left for Australia to work as a journalist. She is in a long-term relationship, but has given Margaret Thatcher no grandchildren. During a period of bad publicity for Mark she jetted in to London to support her mother, but such visits are rare. In 1998, Margaret Thatcher was coming close to regretting the lack of family closeness – so different from her own early childhood above the shop: *All one's thoughts were to have a nice house for the family ... We see them at Christmas. My greatest delight is when my daughter in law sends me photographs of the grandchildren.* But when her interviewer suggested she had paid for her professional success by losing contact with her children she backtracked: *Look, you can't have everything. It has been the greatest privilege being Prime Minister of my country ... Yes I wish I saw more of my children ... And I haven't lost my children. They have their own lives. I took a different life.*[5] And indeed she may not have known or expected anything else. She was certainly Alfred Roberts' favourite daughter, and included in his daily life as a child. But there are few pictures of her children with their grandparents. If a grandmother or grandfather on either side had been available, would the children have gone to boarding school so early? When talking about women entering work, she also talked about the need for another carer – in her childhood, there was a grandmother and the shop workers to help with the two girls.

She did have Denis' constant company and support. But in 2003 Denis Thatcher died. They had been married for 52 years, and he had been her constant companion. By this time, she was less visible on the public stage. On 22 March 2002 she was told by her doctors to make no more public speeches on health grounds, having suffered several small strokes which left her in a very frail state and possibly affected her short-term memory. This must have come as a shock to her – she had always enjoyed remarkably good health. In June 2004 she lost her friend Ronald Reagan. Although she was able to attend the funeral her eulogy for him was pre-taped to prevent undue stress. While this is written, in 2006, she has not appeared in public for a long time, and her public statements are few and far between. She no longer lives in Dulwich, but she is still accompanied by her 24-hour bodyguard. She is 81 years old, and has lived through and been at the centre of eight decades of change in Britain and in British society.

On first leaving Downing Street though, she set herself three goals. First, she intended to travel widely and lecture, particularly in America. She wanted to continue to spread her gospel, but she also wanted to make money. Denis Thatcher was a rich man, but Margaret Thatcher had taken a reduced salary as prime minister for 11 years. Her pension was only £25,000, her MP's salary £21,000.[6] She had an office allowance and an allowance for London members, but this was not enough to support a Central London home and the office staff she needed. John Major awarded all former prime ministers an allowance, and this helped. She signed on for the Washington Speakers' Bureau for a reported fee of $50,000 a lecture – second only to Reagan – and she commanded similar fees in Japan and the Far East. She would not accept payment for speaking politically instead of speaking just as herself – she wished to retain her autonomy in Britain, Russia, China, Hong Kong – anywhere she felt she could have influence.

Her second task was to write her memoirs. Initially, her son Mark took on negotiating a publishing deal. He talked

The handbag

'Margaret Thatcher ... carried the authority of her office always with her. It was in her handbag,' Douglas Hurd said in an interview in 1996. 'No wonder some ministers were actually physically sick before going to meetings with a piece of business likely to be on the receiving end of the most famous handbag in world political history. Julian Critchley cannot have known quite what he was starting when he wrote as early as 1982 that "She cannot see an institution without hitting it with her handbag."'

Mrs Thatcher was both self-aware and quite unrepentant about these traits. On one occasion she opened a ministerial meeting by banging the celebrated bag on the table and declaring *Well, I haven't much time today, only enough time to explode and have my way!* And when she failed to get her way she was furious. *Why* won't *they do what I want them to?*, she fumed to a member of the Cabinet Secretariat once ministers had left after a particular fractious Cabinet committee meeting.

Mrs Thatcher had no idea of what it was like to be on the receiving end of that handbag and the cumulative resentment it could generate, to the point where some, even some of the other big beasts in the ministerial jungle (Heseltine in 1986, Lawson in 1989 and Howe in 1990), could take it no more. Howe, whom (according to Lawson) she 'treated as a cross between a doormat and a punchbag', said of her outburst in her memoirs against Heseltine's alleged breach of collective responsibility over Westland: 'Coming from the past mistress at marginalising Cabinet committees and deciding issues in bilaterals, this is quite a statement.' In such matters Mrs Thatcher was quite without self-irony. And she was unrepentant to the end and beyond the end. In her televised memoirs, screened in the autumn of 1993, she was as fiercely a conviction person as she had been when talking to Kenneth Harris over fourteen years earlier. *I think sometimes the Prime Minister should be intimidating,* she told Denis Blakeway.

[Peter Hennessy: *The Prime Minister* (Penguin, London: 2000), p 401f] about getting even as much as £20 million from the deal, but that fell through. In the end, she sold them for £3.5 million and the two volumes were completed in 1993 and 1995. While she announced that she would write every word herself, this was never a likely possibility. Even so, completing two volumes of political history was a phenomenal challenge. She saw it as a chance to state her case and defend her record. The resulting volumes are detailed chronicles of a life in politics – sometimes, like Margaret Thatcher herself, so bound up in the detail of the individual trees that the broad forest becomes obscure.

Her third project was to set up some sort of institution to preserve her name and propagate her ideas. The Thatcher Foundation was originally intended to be modelled on the Konrad Adenauer Foundation, but in 1991 the British Charity Commissioners refused to grant it charitable status because the organisation was fundamentally political. This limited the opportunities for funding, as rich benefactors were reluctant to give to an institution where they could not receive tax relief. Regardless, a prestigious office was opened near Hyde Park Corner, with an imposing room for Margaret Thatcher to meet foreign visitors. Branches were opened in Washington and Warsaw with the intention of spreading free-market ideas and western business practices. The results have been small. It has evolved into an educational trust, endowing a chair of Enterprise Studies at Cambridge and funding the creation of a CD rom archive of Margaret Thatcher's speeches to be circulated to all British university libraries. It also supports small numbers of Russian students to study business in England for short periods.

She was unable to refrain from public contact with the Conservative Party. She had supported John Major in public, but in private she became outspoken in her disappointment with his policies. For his part, he was a very different operator from his predecessor. He negotiated, quietly and patiently and without loud statements. He won the next election, in 1992, with a reasonable majority, but the party was dogged by dissent over Europe, and lost the 1997 election to Tony Blair. Major stood down, and Margaret Thatcher supported William Hague. When Hague was defeated in the election of 2001, she supported Iain Duncan Smith. But her support was often seen as a liability, and she was changing. It may have been the strokes, or it may have been simply a result of 11 years of political pressure, but her statements were becoming more and more extreme. In *Statecraft – Strategies for a Changing World*, written in 2002, her written statements are far from her beliefs during her own period of responsibility for foreign policy. Dedicated to Ronald Reagan 'to whom the world owes so much' the book is a catalogue of free market, individualistic foreign policies, heavily slanted in support of America and heedless of international law.

The world in which she operated was also changing. In 1979, Britain was tired of strikes and hardship, three-day weeks and collective bargaining. Margaret Thatcher swept into power without having yet explained or demonstrated her particular brand

William Hague first came to Margaret Thatcher's attention in 1977 when at the age of 16 he spoke at the Conservative Party conference, warning that his generation would have to live with the consequences of a Labour government. He entered Parliament in 1989, and in 1995 John Major appointed him Welsh Secretary. Leader of the Conservative Party from 1997 to 2001, he performed well against Blair in the Commons but made little positive impression in the country as a whole. In December 2005 Hague returned to the front bench as Shadow Foreign Secretary under David Cameron.

of individualistic conservatism. Her personal popularity was buoyed up by success in the Falklands, and possibly by her success in reducing strikes. She was the centre of her policies, the figurehead of change. She willingly took the personal stands that connected her to the process of change. And the changes caused great hardship among some sections of British society – hardship that was also visibly linked with the beautifully-dressed Conservative lady with no understanding of poverty. Her record shows that she did listen and change her policies, and not always for the better. The sale of council houses has arguably been the cause of more social division than any other post-war policy, and she initially opposed it. But she said that she didn't listen, she said that she wouldn't turn, she said that her way was the only way and the best way, and so she became absolutely linked with her 11 years of government, years that had seen riots, pitched battles with strikers, record numbers of bankruptcies and house repossessions, and war. She has become more and more linked with memories of disruption and pain – in Tony Blair's England, after 1997, the voters want peace. Her place in the public mind could be summed up by the story of her statue. Eight feet high and cast in white marble, its was to stand in the House of Commons. Five months after it was unveiled, an unemployed man decapitated it.

Nor has she hidden away – in 1998, she made a highly-publicised and controversial visit to the former Chilean dictator Augusto Pinochet during the time he was under house arrest in London facing charges of torture, conspiracy to torture and conspiracy to murder, and expressed her support and friendship for him. She has made several high-profile visits to America, and was an outspoken critic of government policy in the Balkans. She spoke all around the world, and during the Conservative election campaign in 2001. She remains involved with various Thatcherite groups, including being President of the Conservative Way Forward group (who held a dinner at the Savoy Hotel in honour of the 25th Anniversary of her election). She is honorary president of the Bruges Group, which takes its name from the 1988 speech at Bruges where she was first voice her hostility to developments in the European Union.

Her immediate legacy to John Major was a mixed gift. Britain was engaged in the Gulf War abroad, and enmeshed in the Poll Tax at home. The Gulf war ended in February 1991. It could be argued that if she had still been at the helm she could have influenced America more. As it is, in 2006 Britain is occupying Iraq. Michael Heseltine, who had resigned from the Cabinet before the Poll Tax was introduced, was put in charge of creating a new system. The result was a compromise between using national and local authority taxation to fund local services, a compromise that will not have pleased Margaret Thatcher. Her European legacy was almost as difficult. The European Union has been, and still is, the most divisive issue within the Conservative Party. Margaret Thatcher held one pole of the argument – that the EU's function was as a free trade area, and that any closer links between nations in social policy or human rights were an infringement of British sovereignty. The opposing view was that European Union was an absolute advantage to Britain, and that harmonisation of policies could only be of benefit to the British. John Major attempted to steer a middle path. He placed Britain at the heart of Europe, but did not allow that to mean harmonisation. There were 'opt-out' clauses to minimum wage clauses and to the social chapter – both of which will have pleased Margaret Thatcher.

She herself named six 'lessons' that she regarded as the most important of this century, and on which she claimed success.[7] The first lesson was the 'power of ideas', and here her influence on current politics and social life is enormous. She set out, consciously and intentionally, to wean British society away from the princi- ples of equality and collectiv- ism that formed the post-war consensus. In this she changed the political agenda of both the Conservative Party and the Labour Party. In a memorial lecture for Keith Joseph she said: *Creativity is necessarily a quality which pertains to individuals. Indeed, perhaps the one immutable law of anthropology is that we are all different. Now, of course, individuals can't fulfill their potential without a society in which to do so. And to set the record straight – once again – I have never minimised the importance of society, only contested the assumption that society means the State rather than other people.*[8]

I have never minimised the importance of society, only contested the assumption that society means the State rather than other people.

THATCHER

Fundamental to her ideology, before even monetarism or beating inflation – was the belief that individual people should have control over their own finances, their own lives, their own future. People should have the ability to fail in order to have the incentive to work – and the role of the government was to create space for individual choices. This is a moral statement – in her view a healthy society was made up of healthy individuals taking care of their own needs. The post-war consensus, Labour as well as Conservative, believed that a healthy society was made up of individuals rendered free from the fear of want and unemployment, and so free to support each other and their government. Margaret Thatcher saw the shift in the agenda herself: *The sharp divide between the forces of freedom represented by the Conservative Party and the West on the one hand, and the forces of collectivism represented by the Labour Party and the Soviet bloc on the other, is a thing of the past. The extent of the success we achieved in the 1980s has, in this sense, caught up with us.*[9] Certainly, it has caught up with the modern political agenda. It is, of course, a judgment about human nature – which world would people rather live in – a collectivist or an individualistic one? – believing, as Margaret Thatcher and Nye Bevan both believed, that ideology would affect individual behaviour.

Margaret Thatcher's crusade to win hearts and minds was carried out with an unprecedented personal publicity campaign. Perhaps without her influence it would have been harder for Tony Blair to appear on *Parkinson* in 2006. She made the message personal – during her second term, it could be said that the message was so personal it could not be separated from her. Much has been made of her comment when Mark Thatcher provided her with a grandson – *We have become a grandmother of a grandson called Michael*[10] – with its overtones of royalty. Certainly she saw herself as on a mission, and as a true evangelical, saving the British people from the forces of evil. She stood out and stood up for her beliefs, and earned votes and admiration for her stand. She joked about this: *I was just reminded of a cartoon when I came back from the last, uh, summit meeting in Rome. It was a cartoon of eleven men going one way round an athletics track. And me going the other. What the cartoonist didn't know was that he had got the eleven going the* wrong way round *and me going the right way*.[11] That individualism supported by electoral success marks Margaret Thatcher out from other politicians and personalises her legacy. Today I hear students say 'I love Margaret Thatcher' without considering her policies or the practical legacy of those policies.

The legacy of her policies shapes the experience of living in Britain today. There is a growing gap between rich and poor, with unemployment highest (15 per cent) among people of Pakistani and Bangladeshi origin. This does not give a picture of local differences. In London, the borough of Newham has the highest unemployment rate in the country at 38.6 per cent: Bromley has the lowest in London, at 16.7 per cent. The North-East, home of closed steel and coal works, has 25 per cent unemployment.[12] Benefit cuts designed to remove single people of working age and young people from entitlement to unemployment benefit have never been reversed – current policy, to increase the numbers of young people over 17 in higher education hides some of the numbers affected. Sale of council houses has put pressure on any other form of social housing. House prices are high. The result of all this – all measures traceable to Thatcher's budgets – is to make it difficult to escape from poverty. This was not the intention – the intention was that people would develop the entrepreneurial skills to change their situation. But the intention was forged in the middle-class suburbs of a country town, where social mobility was really only gained by a small group of people. The intention was that growing prosperity would result in the prosperous supporting the needy. This has not been the case in any significant way.

Her second lesson – *We now know that it is not government, but free enterprise, which is capable of creating wealth, providing jobs and raising living standards*[13] – is a familiar rallying cry. The idea that the state should be rolled back, and that individuals were responsible for meeting their own social and welfare needs was forged in Grantham, where charity was given through local agencies and in her experience no one starved. It has not proved true in every day experience today. Perhaps the easiest example lies in housing, where the removal of one million houses from public provision should have sparked a vibrant market in low cost sale and rental housing. This has not happened. Social housing – rental housing for the poor – is now usually provided through registered social landlords, often charities. House prices are high, and first time buyers can be priced out of new housing. Government intervention has been necessary to introduce 'share buying' and ensure low-cost homes. Nor have living standards risen for the whole population. In 1999, 26 per cent of the population was living in poverty. In 1979, when Margaret Thatcher came to power, the percentage was 13 per cent. Welfare initiatives designed to cut welfare dependency have increased actual poverty. Groups of claimants removed from the right to benefit during the Thatcher years, 17–18 year olds, strikers, have not been reinstated. The introduction of loans through the Social Fund to the poorest people on Income Support has not been reversed. The intention of these measures was to introduce individual accountability and to reduce what Margaret Thatcher saw as an attitude of reliance on the state. If initiative was rewarded with a job and hard work, then everyone could succeed. Perhaps the message has been more successful than the policy – In 2003 the poorest fifth of the population had a median income of £128 a week. The richest fifth had a median income of nearly five times as much, at £616.[14] Rich and poor are clustered geographically: The loss of Britain's industrial base in the North, and lack of availability of cheap housing, mean that poverty affects whole communities rather than individuals. The practical result of her actions has been to make it harder for people to move out of poverty, and to increase the gap between the rich and poor.

We now know that it is not government, but free enterprise, which is capable of creating wealth, providing jobs and raising living standards.

THATCHER

Her strongest legacy is perhaps in her third lesson. *Third, there is the need for strong defence. And this, of course, is something which is the ultimate test of any government. One lesson from this century's wars cannot be misunderstood: it is that credible deterrence works to keep the peace – and that it is weakness, not strength, which tempts the aggressor.*[15] Margaret Thatcher was instrumental in the resolution of the Cold War between the Soviet Bloc and the United States of America. This does not mean that there is no longer any tension between East and West, but it does mean that Europe in general, and Britain in particular, is no longer squeezed between two nuclear powers. Of course the theatre of war has moved – and perhaps the nuclear stalemate that marked the post-war years would have ended any way. The Thatcher legacy was to introduce change by lauding and exporting free-market values with evangelistic fervour. Her understanding of the power of ideas led her to lead this change with the struggle for hearts and minds. Canvassing for the free market, as she did publicly in Yugoslavia and Moscow and privately in talks with the Soviet Union, was both a courageous and an evangelistic thing to do.

Her government also saw the end of white rule in Rhodesia. From the vantage point of 2006 we may regret Robert Mugabe's hold on power and his treatment of the country, but he first came to power in a free election brought about by British intervention. In a similar way, her government negotiated the handover of Hong Kong, and the protection of capitalism there. The Anglo-Irish Agreement laid the bare foundations for the current cease-fire. In all these places, Margaret Thatcher and her government took decisive action, and carried through a clear programme. The end result, from a 2006 perspective is not always what she intended, but there has been a result that has changed the

One lesson from this century's wars cannot be misunderstood: it is that credible deterrence works to keep the peace – and that it is weakness, not strength, which tempts the aggressor.

THATCHER

course of international relations. A less successful legacy lies with Europe. There, her intransigent refusal to consider closer union damaged Britain's ability to influence decision making for many years. It also polarised opinion in the Conservative Party itself, giving a focus for an argument that has torn the party apart through succeeding time in government and in opposition.

Her fourth lesson was a different one, and one that did not figure largely during her government. *The Twentieth Century will be looked back on as perhaps the only time in the history of our civilisation when some people imagined they could successfully run an economy and sustain a society with weak families.*[16] The view of the family that she expressed throughout her life was an extension of her view of individual rights and responsibilities. The family was the fundamental unit of society, where values were learnt and put into practice. She did not provide support for families through policy because the best interests were served by allowing men and women, fathers and mothers, the opportunity to provide for themselves. She did ensure that young people did not have incentive to leave home because of benefit or housing opportunities. She frowned on the economic and social costs of single parenthood. She said: *The family does not need some special raft of subsidies and privileges to stay afloat. Instead, we must give back to families power and responsibility. And remember: it is through the family that one generation gives the benefit of its wisdom to the next.* The effect of her policies was to increase the responsibility placed on families without providing support. It was the attitude of the middle class families of a small town, with no awareness of the realities of life without money or outside help. Closure of long-stay hospitals shows this very clearly. When her government introduced the National Health Service and Community Care Act in 1990 the intentions included reducing local authority spending and encouraging local authorities to use other organisations to provide services. The effect was to return long-stay patients to their homes or communities. Women bore the brunt of this as carers in the home or low-paid carers in the community, and families were at the forefront of new provision.

In her fifth lesson she returned to familiar ground. *Let us never forget that stability and freedom depend upon popular loyalties to traditional institutions. And the most powerful and pervasive traditional institution which the political world has known is the nation.*[17] She used as illustration the example of communist Russia, where the re-establishment of nation states has been accompanied by war, poverty, and sickness. And in her sixth and final lesson she drew attention to the *Value and Vitality* of the Westminster parliament: *Let us renew our resolve that the sovereignty of the Westminster parliament will never be lightly relinquished; that the sacrifices and struggles of previous generations which won that sovereignty will not be forgotten; and that we will never grow weary or become complacent when the inestimable advantage of being ruled under laws made by our own representatives in our own parliament is put at risk.*[18] She opposed Scots and Welsh devolution, where local parliaments are now in place. But the lasting legacy of her government has been the dissolution of the Conservative Party as a force for effective opposition over the last 15 years.

She was the first woman prime minister of a Western power. Regardless of her own lessons this could have been her biggest legacy – awareness of the potential for women to lead. She was careful of her appearance and her profile, and used her femininity when needed. She came to power at the same time that Women's liberation and second wave feminism were forces for social change. Equal Pay acts and Sexual Discrimination acts were new on the statute book when she was first elected in 1979. She was clear that being a woman had influenced her career – in her memoirs she discusses being selected for Dartford because she was a woman: *Why not take the risk of adopting young Margaret Roberts? There was not much to lose, and some good publicity for the party to win.*[19]

She was clear that there were different expectations, and different standards, because she was a woman. She was interviewed with Barbara Castle and Shirley Williams about the implications of being a woman in Parliament and having to order men about. She said: *I think they're [women] less self-confident than men. That's often struck me. I think a number of women would hold back and say, 'I don't know enough about it' when on the same amount of knowledge, a man would jump in and make quite an inflamed and passionate speech about it and he would know no more relevant facts than the woman who refused to make a speech.*[20] In the same interview, she talked about being visible as a woman in the House, and staying on the benches so that people would see women were represented. But she made no attempt to encourage women into her Cabinet. Almost no women joined her in government, and her close friends and allies were men. Her secretaries and personal assistants were women, but when it came to government her rhetoric was contradicted by her behaviour: *Oh, I do wish we could get more women into Parliament. First, it would make those of us who are there less conspicuous, and that would be a great advantage, but you know, there are not any more really than there were in the 1930s, and it is a great disappointment because women, as I say, are very able. It is partly, I think, that they prefer getting things done rather than making speeches about it and I notice that when women are in Parliament they are extremely practical about how they can move things forward, extremely good constituency members, extremely good on committee work because there we are dealing with the detail, and they are very good at getting down to their homework and knowing all the facts, and really saying: 'But it is no good talking general principles, it is how this applies. Look at how it applies to my constituency.' And yes, we want double, treble, quadruple the numbers. Let us make a target first of having a third of the House of Commons consisting of women. That would be terrific and it would alter things, I think, quite a bit.*[21]

This was a huge disappointment to burgeoning feminists. Although they were ready to support her election at first, her policies about the family, her use of her gender and looks to get results, and her failure to pay any attention to equal rights legislation left many women disappointed. She did offer a role model, but it was one based on individual success in a public world, where private concerns like childcare were individual problems to be solved individually. The result may have been to politicise many women – faced with a feminine role-model with little interest in their concerns, perhaps it was necessary to defeat Thatcherism in order to reclaim equal opportunities.

And what of monetarism? The financial strategy that was worth increasing unemployment and civil unrest for? The belief system that gave an economic foundation for individualistic ideology? As Margaret Thatcher said when describing herself and Ronald Reagan: *Our belief in the virtues of hard work and enterprise led us to cut taxes. Our belief in private property led to the sale of state industries and 'public' housing back to the people. Our belief in sound money led to the monetarist policies that attacked inflation. Our belief in individual initiative over bureaucratic control led to the successful deregulation of finance and industry. And, taken together, all these policies led to a freer society and the greatest period of uninterrupted growth in our history.* Certainly, there has been no return, even wistfully, to Keynesian economics. The introduction of the free market in the health service and education has not been reversed. The privatisation of industry and business continues. Control of the money supply though control of government spending is as much a matter of political consensus as collectivism was before 1979. However, monetarism alone did not destroy inflation. There is also no easy return to monetarist policies.

So what has she left behind? First, an image of personalised, individualistic evangelistic determination that is larger than life. Sometimes loved, often hated, it is impossible to be indifferent to this image. At her best, she was brave to a fault, honest and very feminine – the image of her, perfectly composed and coiffured, on the conference platform after the Brighton bomb is as lasting an image as any picture of wartime bravery. At worst, the same determination and perfect image walked across picket lines and into scenes of disruption and poverty without turning a hair. For women especially this is a mixed gift. While it is absolutely clear that women can take the public space that she took, it would be a brave woman who risked the negative pictures she has left behind. Second, she turned post-war Britain away from collectivism and socialism in ways that cannot easily be reversed. Industries now privatised, welfare benefits re-designed, state housing almost destroyed are not the strongest example of this. The strongest example is a shift in hearts and minds that she would be heartily proud of, that makes socialism seem monstrous and low taxation desirable in the electoral mind. But she did not go as far as she would have liked. She failed to prune public spending with lasting effect, she failed to reduce the Civil Service. Third, she laid the foundations of Britain's close relationship with America. In doing so, she may have irrevocably damaged Britain's future in Europe. Finally, she adopted a presidential approach to government that permitted Parliament and the Shadow Cabinet to blame her for unpopular decisions, even when they would have supported them. This foreshadows Tony Blair's current leadership style, dependent as it is on the personality and celebrity of the leader.

The size and shadow of her legend as an individualistic politician makes the divide between those who love her and those who hate her one of fervour rather than sense. As Andrew Anthony said, 'Thatcher herself remains one of the few political symbols guaranteed to separate us into the ideological tribes of left and right: in the one instance with a kind of visceral loathing, in the other a braying pride.'[22] But the practical and economic result of her one-woman crusade, carried out with courage and skill as well as obstinacy and impatience, has been to change the landscape of British politics, British expectations, and British daily life in as radical a way as Attlee's post-war government introduced collectivism.

NOTES

Chapter 1: Mr Roberts' Daughter

1. Margaret Thatcher, *The Path to Power* (HarperCollins, Oxford: 1995) p 3, hereafter *The Path to Power*.
2. *The Path to Power*, p 5.
3. *The Path to Power*, pp 23–4.
4. *The Path to Power*, p 24
5. Quoted in *The Path to Power*, p 7.
6. *The Path to Power*, p 31.

Chapter 2: Transitions

1. Hugo Young, *'One of Us': a biography of Margaret Thatcher* (Macmillan, London: 1989) p 16.
2. Young, *'One of Us'*, p 16.
3. *The Path to Power*, p 40.
4. Hartmut Kopsch, 'The Approach of the Conservative Party to Social Policy during World War II', unpublished University of London Phd. Thesis, 1974.
5. *The Path to Power*, p 44.
6. *The Path to Power*, p 77.
7. *The Path to Power*, p 96.

Chapter 3: Taking on the Party

1. *The Path to Power*, p 106.
2. Denis Healey, *The Time of my Life* (Michael Joseph, London: 1989) p 487.
3. Quoted in J Campbell, *Margaret Thatcher Vol.1.The Grocer's Daughter* (Jonathan Cape, London: 2000) p 129.
4. Quoted in Campbell, *The Grocer's Daughter*, p 135.

5. House of Commons, 19 April 1961 [Vol.638, cols.1226–32].
6. Jean Mann, *Women in Parliament* (Odhams: 1962) p 31.
7. *Daily Telegraph* 23 October 1969.
8. Margaret Thatcher, *The Downing Street Years* (HarperCollins, London: 1993) p 423, hereafter *The Downing Street Years*.
9. Hugo Young and Anne Sloman, *The Thatcher Phenomenon* (1986) p 23.
10. Speech opening a Conservative fashion show, 2 October 1963, reported in *Finchley Press*, 11 October 1963.
11. Russell Lewis, *Margaret Thatcher* (Routledge and Kegan Paul, London: 1975) p 32.
12. Margaret Thatcher: complete public statements 1945–1990. Database and Compilation © OUP 1999. This title contains material reproduced by consent of Baroness Thatcher, HMSO, and other owners listed on the disk. UDN: 62_015 19 March 1962 – Speech to Finchley Conservatives.
13. *The Path to Power*, p 136.
14. Margaret Thatcher: complete public statements 1945–1990. Database and Compilation © OUP 1999. This title contains material reproduced by consent of Baroness Thatcher, HMSO, and other owners listed on the disk. UDN: 66_022.
15. *The Path to Power*, p 139.
16. Margaret Thatcher: complete public statements 1945–1990. Database and Compilation © OUP 1999. This title contains material reproduced by consent of Baroness Thatcher, HMSO, and other owners listed on the disk. UDN: 84_280 Madge Green, *Woman's Weekly*. The interview was published on 6 July 1985.
17. *The Path to Power*, p 155.

18. Young, *'One of Us'*, p 69.
19. BBC radio interview, 28 November 1974.
20. *The Path to Power*, p 213.

Chapter 4: Thatcher Emerging

1. R Blake, *The Conservative Party from Peel to Major* (Heineman, London: 1997) p 300.
2. *The Path to Power*, p 307.
3. Given in Campbell, *The Grocer's Daughter*, p. 348.
4. *The Path to Power*, p 308.
5. Campbell, *The Grocer's Daughter*, p 352.
6. Quoted in Campbell, *The Grocer's Daughter*, p 352.
7. John O'Sullivan, NRO *Sir Denis, R.I.P. A prince among supporting players dies.* June 27, 2003, 9:45 a.m. http://www.nationalreview.com/jos/jos062703.
8. Campbell, *The Grocer's Daughter*, p 354.
9. *The Path to Power*, p 294.
10. *The Path to Power*, p 311.
11. Campbell, *The Grocer's Daughter*, p 353.
12. *The Path to Power*, p 404.
13. Speech for Conference for Management in Industry, 9 January 1978.
14. Campbell, p 362.

Chapter 5: Thatcherism at Home

1. 4 May 1979 – remarks on entering Downing Street. Margaret Thatcher: complete public statements 1945–1990. Database and Compilation © OUP 1999. This title contains material reproduced by consent of Baroness Thatcher, HMSO, and other owners listed on the disk. UDN: 79_240.
2. *The Downing Street Years*, p 26.
3. *The Downing Street Years*, p 27.

4. *The Downing Street Years*, p 28.

5. *The Downing Street Years*, p 28.

6. *The Downing Street Years*, p 23.

7. House of Commons 15 May 1979 [Vol.967, cols. 73–87].

8. *The Downing Street Years*, p 122; Campbell, p 168.

9. Young, *'One of Us'*, p 83.

10. Quoted in J Campbell, *Margaret Thatcher Vol 2: The Iron Lady* (Jonathan Cape, London: 2003), p 168, hereafter Campbell Vol 2.

11. Carol Thatcher, *Below the Parapet: The Biography of Denis Thatcher* (HarperCollins, London: 1997), p 201.

12. *The Downing Street Years*, p 342.

13. IRN interview, 28 November 1980.

14. Speech to Conservative Rally in Harrogate, 9 June 1987.

15. Campbell, p 374.

16. *The Downing Street Years*, p 414.

17. House of Commons, 30 October 1990 [Vol 178, cols 869–92].

18. Quoted in Campbell, Vol 2, p 721.

Chapter 6: Thatcher Abroad

1. Speech at 'Youth for Europe' Rally, 2 June 1979.

2. *The Downing Street Years*, p 64.

3. Young, *'One of Us'*, p 187.

4. Interview for *The New Yorker*, 30 September 1985.

5. *The Downing Street Years*, p 74.

6. Speech to Mid-Bedfordshire Conservatives, 30 April 1982.

7. *The Downing Street Years*, p 157.

8. Young, *'One of Us'*, p 347.

9. Radio interview (phone-in) for the BBC World Service, 30 October 1983.
10. Interview for *The Daily Mail*, 4 November 1983.
11. House of Commons Statement, 15 April 1986.
12. Interview for *The New Yorker*, 30 September 1985.
13. Campbell, Vol 2, p 283.
14. Campbell, Vol 2, p 296.
15. Campbell, Vol 2, p 298.
16. Interview for *The New Yorker*, 30 September 1985.
17. Sir Robert Renwick, interviewed on 'The Last Europeans', Channel 4, 1995.
18. Radio interview (phone-in) for the BBC World Service, 30 October 1983.
19. Press conference in Hong Kong, 4 December 1984.
20. It is likely that responsibility for this lay with the Irish National Liberation Army rather than the IRA.
21. Speech at Kensington Town Hall, 19 January 1976.
22. Campbell, Vol 2, p 420.
23. Quoted in Garrett Fitzgerald, *All In A Life* (Macmillan, London: 1991) p 261.
24. 22 May 1980, Joint written statement after Anglo-Irish Talks, *The Times*. Margaret Thatcher: complete public statements 1945–1990. Database and Compilation © OUP 1999. This title contains material reproduced by consent of Baroness Thatcher, HMSO, and other owners listed on the disk. UDN: 80_121.
25. Letter to the Reverend Ian Paisley, Anglo-Irish Summit, 10 December 1980.
26. TV interview for BBC, 28 May 1981.
27. Campbell, Vol 2, p 431.
28. *The Downing Street Years*, p 380.
29. *The Downing Street Years*, p 382.
30. Campbell, Vol 2, p 434.

Chapter 7: After Thatcher

1. *The Downing Street Years*, p 860.
2. *The Downing Street Years*, p 861.
3. Interview for *Women's Own*, 23 September 1987.
4. *Daily Express*, 7 December 2005.
5. *Saga Magazine*, 28 August 1998.
6. Campbell, Vol 2, p 755.
7. Margaret Thatcher Speech receiving Freedom of City of Westminster, 12 December 1990.
8. Keith Joseph Memorial Lecture, 11 January 1996. Margaret Thatcher: complete public statements 1945–1990. Database and Compilation © OUP 1999. This title contains material reproduced by consent of Baroness Thatcher, HMSO, and other owners listed on the disk. UDN: 96_001.
9. Keith Joseph Memorial Lecture, 11 January 1996. Margaret Thatcher: complete public statements 1945–1990. Database and Compilation © OUP 1999. This title contains material reproduced by consent of Baroness Thatcher, HMSO, and other owners listed on the disk. UDN: 96_001.
10. 3.03.89 Remarks outside Downing Street, 3 March 1989.
11. Speech to Finchley Conservatives, 10 November 1990.
12. Figures from National Statistics Office, http://www.statistics.gov.uk, visited 31 March 2006.
13. Margaret Thatcher Speech receiving Freedom of City of Westminster, 12 December 1990.
14. Child Poverty Action Group – 'Poverty, the Facts'.
15. Margaret Thatcher Speech receiving Freedom of City of Westminster, 12 December 1990.
16. Margaret Thatcher Speech receiving Freedom of City of Westminster, 12 December 1990.

17. Margaret Thatcher Speech receiving Freedom of City of Westminster, 12 December 1990.
18. Margaret Thatcher Speech receiving Freedom of City of Westminster, 12 December 1990.
19. *The Path to Power*, p 64.
20. Interview for BBC Radio 4 'Analysis', 14 January 1972.
21. Interview for Central TV, 18 June 1986.
22. Andrew Anthony, 'Thatcher's legacy: no more Us and Them', *The Guardian* 5 May 2004.

CHRONOLOGY

Year	Premiership
1979	4 May: Margaret Thatcher becomes Prime Minister, aged 53. European Elections. Lusaka Commonwealth Meeting began (ended 8 August). IRA murders Mountbatten and 18 soldiers (Warrenpoint). Exchange controls abolished. Dublin European Council: budget row begins. USSR invades Afghanistan.
1980	Steel strike begins (ends 3 April). Cabinet agrees European budget proposal; short-term settlement. Iran-Iraq war begins. Reagan elected US President
1981	NCB announces pit closures (abandoned 18 February). Second Republican hunger strike begins in Northern Ireland (ends 3 October). Budget: counter-Keynesian – increases taxes at bottom of depression. Social Democratic Party (SDP) formed ('Alliance' of SDP & Liberals, 16 June). Crosby by-election: Shirley Williams wins Conservative seat for SDP

History	Culture
USA and China open diplomatic relations.	Judy Chicago, *The Dinner Party*.
European Monetary System becomes operational.	Alban Berg, *Lulu*.
Iran is declared an Islamic Republic by Ayatollah Khomeini.	The Clash, *London Calling*. Boomtown Rats, *I don't like Mondays*.
Carter and Brezhnev sign the SALT II treaty limiting nuclear weapons.	Milan Kundera, *The Book of Laughter and Forgetting*.
Iranian students seize the US embassy in Tehran and demand the return of the Shah for trial.	Peter Schaffer, *Amadeus*. Martin Sherman, *Bent*. Films: *Alien. Mad Max. Manhattan. Monty Python's Life of Brian*. TV: *Antiques Roadshow. Life on Earth. Minder. Tinker, Tailor, Soldier, Spy*.
US ban trade with Iran, break off relations and expel Iranian diplomats.	Richard Rorty, *Philosophy and the Mirror of Nature*.
EC imposes trade sanctions against Iran..	Umberto Eco, *The Name of the Rose*.
OPEC increases crude oil prices by 10 per cent.	Joseph Brodsky, *A Part of Speech*. Mark Medoff, *Children of a Lesser God*. Elliot Carter, *Night Fantasies*. Philip Glass, *Satyagraha* (opera). Cindy Sherman, *Untitled* No. 66. Tony Cragg, *Plastic Pallette I*. Films: *Airplane!. Raging Bull. Tess*.
Greece becomes tenth member of the EC.	Alisdair MacIntyre, *After Virtue*.
François Mitterrand becomes first socialist president of France.	Bucks Fizz win the Eurovision Song Contest for the United Kingdom.
Gunman seriously wounds Pope John Paul II in an assassination attempt.	Films: *Mommie Dearest. The Postman Always Rings Twice. On Golden Pond*.
Israel formally annexes the Golan Heights, occupied in 1967.	TV: *Only Fools and Horses. Brideshead Revisited*.
President Reagan introduces economic sanctions against the USSR.	

Argentina invades Falklands. UN SCR 502 demands Argentine withdrawal; British Task Force sails. South Georgia recaptured Argentine cruiser *General Belgrano* sunk. HMS *Sheffield* hit by Argentine Exocet missile. British Forces land at San Carlos Bay June: Argentine forces on the Falklands surrender.

Reagan announces 'Star Wars' (Strategic Defence Initiative); Thatcher supports.
General election: Conservative Government formed. (144 majority)
US invasion of Grenada.

History	Culture
Spain agrees to end blockade of Gibraltar.	Jenny Holzer, *Times Square*.
Military coup in Guatemala.	Luciano Berio, *La vera Storia*.
Military coup in Bangladesh.	Dire Straits, *Love over Gold*.
Israeli Prime Minister Begin announces that Israel will assert sovereignty over occupied West Bank.	Michael Jackson, *Thriller*.
	Isabel Allende, *The House of Spirits*.
	Primo Levi, *If Not Now, When?*.
Israeli armed forces invade Lebanon.	Julian Mitchell, *Another Country*.
USA announces new Middle East peace proposals, which are rejected by Israel.	Tadeusz Cantor, *The Dead Class*.
	Richard Rorty, *The Consequences of Pragmatism*.
Sikhs besiege Indian Parliament in New Delhi.	Films: *ET. Ghandi. An Officer and a Gentleman*.
President Brezhnev dies.	TV: *Countdown. The Young Ones. Brookside. Boys from the Blackstuff*.
Bombs destroy Israeli HQ in Lebanon.	
IBM produces first PC with in-built hard disk.	Karl Popper, *Realism and the Aim of Science*.
HIV virus isolated.	J M Coetzee, *The Life and Times of Michael K*.
	Alice Walker, *The Colour Purple*.
	Gabriel Garcia Marquez, *Chronicle of a Death Foretold*.
	Oliver Messiaen, *Saint Francois d'Assise* (opera).
	Michael Jackson, *Beat It. Billie Jean*.
	David Bowie, *Let's Dance*.
	Eurythmics, *Sweet Dreams (Are Made of This)*.
	Niki de Saint Phalle/Jean Tingeley, *Fountain*. (Pompidou)
	Cindy Sherman, *Untitled No. 131*.
	Films: *The Dresser. Zelig*.
	TV: *The Jewel in the Crown*
	Breakfast television begins in the UK.

Year	Premiership

1984   Miners' strike begins.

Fontainebleau European Council; long-term European budget settlement.

Brighton bomb: failed IRA attempt to assassinate Thatcher and her Cabinet.

Flotation of British Telecom: key privatisation measure.

Gorbachev visits Chequers: Thatcher describes him as a man she can do business with

Hong Kong: Thatcher signs Joint Agreement with China.

1985   NUM votes to end coal strike.

Anglo-Irish Agreement signed at Hillsborough: consultative role for Republic.

Luxembourg European Council; Single European Act agreed.

History	Culture
Brunei becomes independent. Iraq commences bombing Iran. Ronald Reagan (Republican) wins US Presidential election.	Milan Kundera, *The Unbearable Lightness of Being*. Martin Amis, *Money*. Tom Clancy, *The Hunt for Red October*. New edition of James Joyce, *Ulysses* correcting 5,000 errors. Band Aid raises £8 million for Ethiopian famine relief with *Do they know it's Christmas?* Michael Jackson wins eight Grammys. Turner's *Seascape, Folkstone* is auctioned for $10 million. Films: *Amadeus. Paris, Texas.* TV: *The Bill. The Living Planet. Spitting Image.*
Mikhail Gorbachev is named First Secretary of Soviet Communist Party. Shi'ite gunmen hijack TWA aeroplane demanding release of prisoners held in Israel. Explosion sinks Greenpeace ship *Rainbow Warrior*, killing one. First elections held for Hong Kong's legislative council. Palestinian guerrillas hijack an Italian cruise liner. Major famine in Ethiopia.	Habermas, *The Philosophical Discourse of Modernity*. Julian Barnes, *Flaubert's Parrot*. Patrick Süsskind, *Perfume*. Ted Hughes appointed Poet Laureate. Saatchi Collection opens in London. Christo wraps the Pont Neuf, Paris. USA for Africa record *We are the World*. Live Aid rock concert raises more than $60 million for famine relief. Films: *After Hours. Back to the Future.* TV: *Eastenders. The War Game.*

Year	Premiership

1986   Westland: Heseltine walks out of cabinet; replaced at Defence by
George Younger. Brittan resigns, Channon replaces him at DTI
Westland: emergency debate, ending the crisis
US air raids on Libya, mainly from British bases; Thatcher attacked
for allowing them
Anglo-US Summit at Camp David: Thatcher and Reagan issue arms
control statement.

1987   'Louvre Accord' to halt decline in $; Lawson secretly begins
shadowing DM.
Thatcher visits USSR (ended 1 April).
General Election: Conservative Government formed (101 majority).
'Black Monday': Dow Jones falls 23 per cent

History	Culture
Portugal and Spain enter European Community.	Kingsley Amis, *The Old Devils.*
Jacques Chirac is elected Prime Minister of France.	Larry McMurtry, *Lonesome Dove.*
	Musée D'Orsay, Paris is opened.
	Lucien Freud, *Painter and Model.*
Major accident at Chernobyl nuclear power station near Kiev announced.	A Lloyd Webber, *The Phantom of the Opera.*
The seven major Western economic powers hold a summit meeting in Tokyo.	Paul Simon, *Graceland.*
	TV: *The Singing Detective. Casualty. Neighbours* begins on UK television.
Rt Rev Desmond Tutu enthroned as first black Archbishop of Cape Town, SA.	
Reykjavik (Reagan-Gorbachev) Summit; talk of abolishing nuclear weapons	
Iran launches missile attack on Baghdad; Later truce is agreed.	Jacques Derrida, *Of Spirit, Derrida and the Question.*
US President Reagan accepts full responsibility for Iran-Contra scandal..	Tom Wolfe, *Bonfire of the Vanities.*
US destroyers and commandos attack Iranian oil installations in Gulf.	Margaret Atwood, *The Handmaid's Tale.*
US-USSR Summit in Washington. Reagan and Gorbachev agree to eliminate intermediate nuclear forces.	Nigel Osborne, *The Electrification of the Soviet Union.*
	Judith Weir, *A Night at the Chinese Opera.*
World population reaches 5 billion.	Richard Deacon, *The Back of My Hand.*
	Films: *Fatal Attraction. The Last Emperor.*
	TV: *All Creatures Great and Small. Inspector Morse.*

1988   Sterling 'uncapped' on Thatcher's insistence and rises above 3DM.
        Budget: highest rate of income tax cut to 40 per cent.
      Interest rates cut to 7.5 per cent (lowest 1979–90); Thatcher
        publicly supports Lawson.

1989   NHS White Paper published (*Working for Patients*).
      Thatcher clashes with Howe and Lawson on ERM line at Madrid
        Council (met again 25 June).
      Thatcher sets conditions for ERM entry ('Madrid conditions'); reject
        Social Chapter.
      Lawson resigns as Chancellor of the Exchequer; Major replaces him.

History	Culture
Gorbachev announces Soviet withdrawal from Afghanistan from May New York Stock Exchange registers third largest one-day fall in history.	Stephen Hawking, *A Brief History of Time.*
President Mitterand wins French presidential election.	Salman Rushdie, *The Satanic Verses.*
Peace agreement between Somalia and Ethiopia ends 11 years of conflict.	Gabriel Garcia Marquez, *Love in the Time of Cholera.*
Iraq and Iran announce ceasefire.	Thomas Harris, *The Silence of the Lambs.*
Gorbachev is elected President of the USSR by Supreme Soviet.	Gyoergy Ligeti, *Concerto for Piano and Orchestra.*
George Bush wins US presidential election.	Witold Lutoslawski, *Piano Conerto.*
	Anish Kapoor, *Mother as Void.*
	Jasper Johns' *False Start* sold for $17 million.
	Films: *The Last Temptation of Christ. Rain Man.*
	TV: *Red Dwarf.*
Ayatollah Khomeini issues *fatwa* against Salman Rushdie for 'blasphemy' in *The Satanic Verses.*	Kazuo Ishiguro, *The Remains of the Day.*
Tiananmen Square massacre in Beijing.	Anne Tyler, *Breathing Lessons.*
Gorbachev and Kohl sign Bonn Document affirming the right of European sates to determine their own political systems.	Wendy Wasserstein, *The Heidi Chronicles.*
Mass demonstration in Leipzig demands political reform in East Germany.	William Nicholson, *Shadowlands.*
East Germany announces opening of borders with West Germany. Berlin Wall is demolished. Czechoslovakia: end of Communist rule (Havel President 29 December)	I M Pei, *Pyramid* outside the Louvre, Paris.
Romania: dictator Ceausescu overthrown (killed 25 December)	John Cage, *Europera III/IV*
US troops invade Panama to overthrow General Noriega's regime.	A Lloyd Webber, *Aspects of Love.*
	Films: *Batman. When Harry met Sally. Dead Poets' Society.*

Year	Premiership

1990   Trafalgar Square riot against Community Charge ('Poll Tax').

Strangeways prison siege (ends 25 April); disturbances in other gaols.

Ridley resigns over comments on Germany.

Iraq invades Kuwait; Thatcher with Bush in Aspen. UK announces commitment of forces to the Gulf.

Britain joins ERM; interest rates cut by 1 per cent to 14 per cent.

Howe resigns. Howe's resignation speech bitterly critical of Thatcher.

Heseltine stands for Conservative leadership Conservative leadership election first ballot (Thatcher 204: Heseltine 152). Thatcher announces Decision not to contest second ballot.

28 November: Thatcher resigns. After 11 years and 209 days in office, she is the longest-serving Prime Minister of the 20th century.

History	Culture
General Noriega surrenders to US authorities.	Karl Popper, *A World of Propensities.*
President de Klerk ends 30–year ban on ANC. Nelson Mandela is released after 27 years in prison in South Africa.	Martin Amis, *London Fields.*
	Patricia Cornwell, *Post Mortem.*
	Ian McEwan, *The Innocent.*
In East Germany, first free elections since 1933. 'Alliance for Germany' wins 48 per cent of vote.	Derek Wolcott, *Remembrance.*
	Brian Ferneyhough, *String Quartet No. 4.*
Boris Yeltsin elected President of Russian Federation, defeating Gorbachev's candidate.	Gyoergy Ligeti, *Concerto for Violin and Orchestra.*
	Jeff Koons, *Jeff and Ilona.*
East and West Germany sign reunification treaty. GDR ceases to exist.	Damian Hirst, *My Way.*
	Films: *Goodfellas. Cinema Paradiso. Wild at Heart.*
	TV: *Have I Got News For You. One Foot in the Grave. The Trials of Life.*

FURTHER READING

There has been a huge growth of writing about Margaret Thatcher, Thatcherism and Monetarism. I have reduced this list to those books and authors who have contributed to my own understanding of the person and the subject.

Books by the Thatchers

Thatcher, Carol, *Below the Parapet: Biography of Denis Thatcher* (Harper Collins, London: 1997).

———, *Diary of an election: With Margaret Thatcher on the campaign trail* Sidgewick and Jackson, London: 1983).

Thatcher, Margaret, *The Downing Street Years*. (HarperCollins, London: 1993).

———, *The Path to Power* (HarperCollins, London: 1995).

———, *Statecraft: Strategies for a Changing World* (HarperCollins, London: 2003).

Biographies, authorised or otherwise

Abse, L, *Margaret, daughter of Beatrice : a politician's psychobiography of Margaret Thatcher* (Jonathan Cape, London: 1989).

Campbell, J, *Margaret Thatcher Vol.1. The Grocer's Daughter* (Jonathan Cape, London: 2000).

———, *Margaret Thatcher Vol. 2. The Iron Lady* (Jonathan Cape, London: 2003).

Cosgrave, P, *Margaret Thatcher : Prime Minister* (Arrow Books, London: 1978).

Murray, P, *Margaret Thatcher* (W H Allen, London: 1980).

Young, H, *'One of Us': a biography of Margaret Thatcher* (Macmillan, London: 1989).

Books about Thatcherism

Different aspects of Thatcherism have attracted different analyses: it is possible to find writing on almost any aspect of the Thatcher governments or policies or actions. This list is indicative reading including general commentaries as well as specific critiques.

Andrews, K, and J Jacobs, *Punishing the poor: poverty under Thatcher* (Macmillan, London: 1990).

Bagwell, P S, *End of the line?: the fate of public transport under Thatcher* (Verso Editions and NLB, London: 1984).

Byrd, P, *British Foreign Policy under Thatcher* (Philip Allan, Oxford: 1988).

——, *British Defence Policy: Thatcher and beyond*. Philip Allan, New York, London: 1991).

Campbell, B, *The Iron Ladies : why do women vote Tory?* (Virago, London: 1987).

Dalyell, T, *Misrule: how Mrs Thatcher has misled Parliament from the sinking of the Belgrano to the Wright affair* (Hamish Hamilton, London: 1987).

Durham, M, (1991). *Moral Crusades: family and morality in the Thatcher years* (New York University Press, New York: 1991).

Edmonds, J, and Trent Business School, *Trade unions – is there life after Thatcher?* (Trent Business School, Trent Polytechnic, Nottingham: 1987).

Evans, E J, *Thatcher and Thatcherism* (Routledge, London: 1997).

Ewing, K D and C A Gearty, *Freedom under Thatcher: civil liberties in modern Britain* (Clarendon Press, Oxford: 1990).

Ferguson, J, and J Pearce, *The Thatcher years: Britain and Latin America*. (Latin America Bureau, London: 1988).

Gaffikin, F, and M Morrissey, *Northern Ireland: the Thatcher years* (Zed Press, London: 1990).

George, B, S d'Albertanson, et al. (1985). British defence policy, decision making and expenditure under the Thatcher Governments 1979–1985 (and beyond) (International Security Studies Program, Washington DC: 1985).

Jackson, P M, and Royal Institute of Public Administration, *Implementing government policy initiatives: the Thatcher administration 1979–83* (Royal Institute of Public Administration, London: 1985).

James, G, *In the public interest: a devastating account of the Thatcher government's involvement in the covert arms trade, by the man who turned Astra Fireworks into a £100m arms manufacturer* (Warner Books, London: 1996).

Johnson, C, *The economy under Mrs Thatcher 1979–1990* (Penguin, London: 1991).

Joseph, K J, and Centre for Policy Studies, *Monetarism is not enough* (Centre for Policy Studies, Chichester: 1976).

Kavanagh, D, and A Seldon, *The Thatcher Effect* (Clarendon, Oxford: 1989).

Marsh, D, J King, *et al*, *The Trade Unions under Thatcher* (Dept. of Government, University of Essex, Colchester: 1985).

Midwinter, A F and Department of Government, University of Strathclyde, *Public finance in the Thatcher era : a critical assessment* (Dept. of Government, University of Strathclyde, Glasgow: 1992).

Moon, J, *Innovative leadership in democracy: policy change under Thatcher* (Dartmouth, Aldershot: 1993).

Raban, J, *God, Man & Mrs Thatcher* (Chatto & Windus, London: 1989).

Riddell, P, *The Thatcher Government* (Basil Blackwell, Oxford: 1985).

——, *The Thatcher Decade: how Britain has changed during the 1980s* (Basil Blackwell, Oxford: 1989).

——, *The Thatcher era and its legacy* (Basil Blackwell, Oxford: 1991).

Savage, S P and L Robins, *Public policy under Thatcher* (Macmillan, London: 1990).

Thornton, P, and National Council for Civil Liberties, *Decade of decline: civil liberties in the Thatcher years* (National Council for Civil Liberties, London:1989).

Thornton, R C, *The Falklands Sting: Reagan, Thatcher, and Argentina's bomb* (Brassey's, London/Washington DC: 1998).

Urban, G R, *Diplomacy and disillusion at the court of Margaret Thatcher : an insider's view* (I B Tauris, London: 1996).

Wilsher, P, D Macintyre, *et al*, *Strike: Thatcher, Scargill and the miners* (Coronet, Sevenoaks: 1985).

PICTURE SOURCES

Page 2
Mrs Thatcher pauses to wave to her supporters from the
doorstep of Number 10 Downing Street just before entering
as Britain's first ever woman Prime Minister, 5 May 1979.
(Courtesy Topham Picturepoint)

Page 75
On an official visit to the Falkland Islands after the conflict,
Mrs Thatcher examines at close range the heavily mined
Rookery Bay beach, 9 January 1983. (Courtesy Topham
Picturepoint)

Pages 108
Dining at Number 10 Downing Street, Mrs Thatcher
and her closest ally, President Ronald Reagan. (Courtesy
Topham Picturepoint)

INDEX

THE 20 BRITISH PRIME MINISTERS
OF THE 20TH CENTURY

Boxed Set
(all 20 books plus
TIMELINE OF THE
20TH CENTURY
extra and only available
as part of the boxed set):
ISBN 1-904950-53-1